# TO PERFORM
# THE MERCY

# TO PERFORM THE MERCY

Notes on the Liturgy of the 1928 Book of Common Prayer and the 1940 Hymnal and the Canons of the Diocese of the Holy Cross

Paul C. Hewett

*To Perform the Mercy*
Copyright © 2021 by Paul C. Hewett. All rights reserved.

No part of this publication may be reproduced, stored in a retrieval system or transmitted in any way by any means, electronic, mechanical, photocopy, recording or otherwise without the prior permission of the author except as provided by USA copyright law.

The opinions expressed by the author are not necessarily those of URLink Print and Media.

1603 Capitol Ave., Suite 310 Cheyenne, Wyoming USA 82001
1-888-980-6523 | admin@urlinkpublishing.com

URLink Print and Media is committed to excellence in the publishing industry.

Book design copyright © 2021 by URLink Print and Media. All rights reserved.

Published in the United States of America

Library of Congress Control Number: 2021901765
ISBN 978-1-64753-657-2 (Paperback)
ISBN 978-1-64753-658-9 (Digital)

19.01.21

*"To perform the mercy promised to our forefathers,
and to remember his holy covenant…"
Luke 1: 72*

# CONTENTS

Introduction ................................................................... 9

Introductory Material in the Prayer Book ..................... 13

Morning and Evening Prayer ........................................ 17

The Holy Communion and The Collects, Epistles, and Gospels ................................................................... 30

The Collects, Epistles and Gospels ............................... 42

The Ministration of Holy Baptism ................................ 54

The Psalter ................................................................... 63

The Ordinal .................................................................. 66

A Catechism ................................................................. 75

Family Prayer ............................................................... 79

The Articles of Religion ............................................... 82

Notes On Eucharistic Theology And Customs ............. 85

Notes on the 1940 Hymnal ........................................... 92

Canon Law ................................................................. 108

Bibliography .............................................................. 121

# INTRODUCTION

These Notes are for those interested in learning more about Anglican distinctives such as the Book of Common Prayer, and our use of it in worship, "to perform the mercy" of our redemption in Christ. It is hoped that clergy, lay readers and many among the laity will find the background material presented here useful devotionally, and in the celebration of the Liturgy of our Church.

We will be using Massey Shepherd's *Oxford American Prayer Book Commentary* as a primary source. This is sometimes available on line at a reasonable price, but is not necessary to have in using these notes.

The various Books of Common Prayer are, throughout the centuries, in the Church of England, 1549, 1552, 1559, and 1662, and in the U.S., 1789, 1892 and 1928. We will not count late 20th century revisions, as they are more books of alternative services than a Book of Common Prayer. We may keep in mind that those who came from England to settle in the American colonies and Canada brought with them the 1662 Prayer Book, the same Book the Church of England's missionaries used in settling Australia and New Zealand and in evangelizing India, Ceylon and Africa. The 1662 Book of Common Prayer was the theological, liturgical, spiritual and devotional underpinning of the British Empire, the lens through which we read Holy Scripture. It has been said that over 90% of the contents of all editions of the Prayer Book are Holy Scripture, quoted directly or paraphrased. Most phrases of the collects and prayers can be traced to a verse in the Bible. The Prayer Book is indeed the Bible at prayer.

Each subsequent revision in the United States, 1789, 1892 and 1928, was theologically and liturgically, a step by step return to the original 1549 Book, Archbishop Thomas Cranmer's first, and best, edition. Aesthetically, in terms of language, Cranmer's work in translating from the Latin liturgies then in use, and incorporating elements of the 4th century Liturgy of St. John Chrysostom, and some Lutheran elements, has been, through the centuries, an absolute masterpiece. Cranmer (and Myles Coverdale before him, who translated our Prayer Book Psalter) were probably the two most gifted craftsmen of the language in their times.

In the 15th and 16th centuries, as Robert MacNeil has pointed out, the English language was "versatile, highly colored, playful, innovative and self-confident." *(The Story of English,* p. 88) We cannot miss this as we recite the Psalms from Coverdale's 1535 Psalter, or Cranmers Post-communion prayer, cited by an English professor as the greatest prose ever penned in English. Modern prose, by comparison, can be flat, dull and stale, bureaucratic and pedestrian. Someone once said that a confession of sins in modern English sounds like an apology for missing a train. Cranmer's general confessions, in the Daily Office and the Eucharist, hit the nail on the head: "We have left undone those things which we ought to have done; and we have done those things which we ought not to have done, and there is no health in us…"

Speaking of the Daily Office, it was ingenious of Cranmer to re-shape the seven monastic offices into two, Morning and Evening Prayer. The Eucharist is the crown jewel, and every jewel has a setting, and the setting is a two-fold Office in which clergy and laity can take part daily, in church or at home. So the Liturgy is the Eucharist, surrounded by the Daily Offices, augmented by the Litany. And the Prayer Book becomes not just a book of liturgies and prayers, but a Benedictine *Regula*, a Rule, for the ordering of all life, for the sanctification of time, and available to the whole Body of Christ. And in time, Evening Prayer would, in the great cathedrals and parishes throughout England, go on to become *Evensong,* in a cathedral choral tradition unrivaled anywhere in the world.

It is said that the three great classics of the English language are the King James Version of the Bible, the works of William Shakespeare, and the Book of Common Prayer. Familiarity with these classics is essential if we are to have some awareness of who we are as a people in English speaking cultures, and of who we are as sinners, now redeemed in the tender mercies of our God.

And so, in the eloquent and majestic words of the first Exhortation for the Eucharistic Liturgy, we give "most humble and hearty thanks to God, the Father, the Son, and the Holy Ghost, for the redemption of the world by the death and passion of our Saviour Christ, both God and man, who did humble himself, even to the death upon the Cross, for us, miserable sinners, who lay in darkness and the shadow of death, that he might make us the children of God, and exalt us to everlasting life. And to that end we should always remember the exceeding great love of our Master, and only Saviour, Jesus Christ, thus dying for us, and the innumerable benefits which by his precious blood-shedding he hath obtained for us; he hath instituted and ordained holy mysteries, as pledges of his love, and for a continual remembrance of his death, to our great and endless comfort. To him, therefore, with the Father and the Holy Ghost, let us give, as we are most bounden, continual thanks; submitting ourselves wholly to his holy will and pleasure, and studying to serve him in true holiness and righteousness all the days of our life. *Amen."* (p. 86)

# INTRODUCTORY MATERIAL IN THE PRAYER BOOK

**The Title Page**, page Roman numeral i: When the American colonies won their independence from Great Britain, what had been the Church of England in the colonies decided to choose a new name. The Convention that adopted the 1789 Book of Common Prayer (BCP) chose the name "Protestant Episcopal Church in the United States of America." The delegates liked the word "Episcopal," (a church governed by *episkopoi*, bishops) but needed to differentiate themselves from other churches that are governed by bishops, the Roman Catholics and the Orthodox, and the Swedish Lutherans. So they added the word "Protestant," since we are a non-papal church governed by bishops. In those days the word "protestant" had less of a negative connotation (what we are against) and more of a positive meaning, what we are *pro*. We are *pro* the consensus of the undivided Church of the first millennium, the patristic consensus. To *protest* something tended more to mean what you propose and support.

**Page ii has the "Certificate,"** signed by the Custodian of the Standard Book of Common Prayer, "that this edition… has been compared with a certified copy of the Standard Book…" The Standard Book is in a glass case in the Archives of the National Cathedral in Washington, D.C. Every publisher who prints the BCP must ensure that the text, and pagination, is the same as the Standard Book, so that everyone using the Book is "on the same page." It is interesting to note that the Prayer Book is not copyrighted, so that everyone can freely borrow from it at will.

**The Table of Contents** is on page iii. Most of what is listed here is taken from the five medieval books that Archbishop Thomas Cranmer condensed into one volume, the 1549 BCP. These books from antiquity were (a). *the Breviary* (the Daily Office, with the Litany), from p. x to p. 63; (b). *The Missal* (everything pertaining to the Eucharist), pp. 67–269. The Penitential Office, pp. 60-63, could be included in this section, as a preparation for Holy Communion; (c). *The Pastorale* (everything pertaining to sacraments and offices from birth to death), pp. 273 to 342; (d). *The Psalter*, pp. 345 to 525; and (e). the Ordinal (everything pertaining to the ministrations of bishops), pp. 529 to 574. There is a sixth section added later, for the layman's use: the Catechism, and Family Prayer, pp. 577 to 600, and a seventh section, added later, the Articles of Religion, pp. 603 to 611.

**From the Preface**, on p. vi, there is a very significant phrase, toward the end: "…it will also appear that this Church (in the United States) is far from intending to depart from the Church of England in any essential point of doctrine, discipline, or worship; or further than local circumstances require."

What is the significance of this phrase?

In **Concerning the Service of the Church**," on p. vii, it is worth noting that our Liturgy consists of three things together: "The Order for Holy Communion, the Order for Morning Prayer, the Order for Evening Prayer, and the Litany…" Morning Prayer and Evening Prayer can be counted as one thing, the Daily Office. It is a very Benedictine concept to have the Eucharist surrounded by the Daily Offices, as a jewel is surrounded by its setting. As we shall see, one of Cranmer's most brilliant and far reaching reforms is to restore the Daily Offices to the laity, such that they are recited daily in all parish churches, as the context in which the Eucharist is celebrated, all of it dove-tailing together, all of it a means whereby God "performs the mercy" in our midst.

Also on p. vii is "The Use of the Psalter..." There are four ways to use psalms in the daily offices:

(a) as appointed in the Lectionary, pp. x–xlv;
(b) according to the day of the month, as can be seen on p. 345, with "The First Day, Morning Prayer," (Psalms 1-5) and on p. 348, Evening Prayer for the First Day (Psalms 6-8) which seminarians sometimes affectionately call "the Daily Grind," going through all 150 Psalms in a month
(c) using the Selection of Psalms (based on themes) on p. Roman numeral ix
(d) officiant's choice

**A fascinating factoid**–in the early 20th century, there was an annual contest among printers in the United States for the book that had most elegant, most artistic type-setting. The 1928 BCP was submitted in 1928, and won in 1929. There have been members of Protestant denominations — even clergy — who became Anglicans because of this Prayer Book...they said, "these people must know what they believe," with everything presented and layed out with such elegance. Notice how modern revisions have no such elegance...no justified right hand margins...everything is ragged and provisional, with all the harsh, ragged edges of sterile Bauhaus architecture.

**Tables and Rules** on p. li give us times of fasting and abstinence. The introduction to the *St. Augustine's Prayer Book* has some good teaching on this. Fasting is reducing the quantity of food. Abstinence is reducing the quality, sometimes by not eating meat. Those who need not fast are the very young, or old, the sick or infirm, pregnant women, and those whose work is so physical in nature that they must eat heartily, eg, lumberjacks, farmers, miners, athletes, etc.

Even if fasting is beyond us, we can always abstain from something (smoking, drinking, TV, internet games, magazines), and using the time or money saved for devotion or the relief of the needy.

- Ash Wednesday and Good Friday are days of fasting and abstinence.
- Fridays are days of abstinence (Fridays in Lent are days of fasting and abstinence)
- The Forty Days of Lent are for fasting (excepting Sundays)
- Other days of fasting are the Ember Days and the Rogation Days

Regarding the Eucharistic fast, the various dioceses have their own regulations. The author tends to follow modern Roman practice, to fast for at least an hour before the beginning of Mass. For Sunday morning Masses it is possible for those in good health to fast from midnight onwards, so that the Blessed Sacrament is the first food of the day.

- Isaiah 58 is often used as a teaching on real fasting
- As an old saying has it: "prayer sets the nail; fasting drives it home."

# MORNING AND EVENING PRAYER

*together with*
Prayers and Thanksgivings
The Litany
A Penetential Office

This section is what in the middle ages was called the *Breviary*—the Daily Offices, usually, in the Benedictine system, seven in number, if Lauds and Prime are combined: (Mattins, Lauds, Prime, Terce, Sext, None, Vespers and Compline) What Cranmer did was combine Mattins, Lauds and Prime to form Morning Prayer (MP), and Vespers and Compline, to form Evening Prayer (EP).

**Morning Prayer.** The rubrics at the top of p. 3 provide different ways to begin. It is necessary to select only one Opening Sentence, and best to read only one, using the ones for the seasons, as appropriate.

The Exhortation on the bottom of p. 5, which begins "Dearly beloved," should be omitted when Mass follows Morning Prayer, and should be omitted on all but special penitential days. It could be useful when the Congregation has nothing but Morning Prayer and a Lay Reader for Sunday morning. When omitted, we say, on p. 6, "Let us humbly confess…" instead.

The General Confession on p. 6 should be omitted when Mass follows Morning Prayer. When there is daily Morning and Evening Prayer, the confession is usually used only at Evening Prayer.

The Absolution on p. 7 will of course be omitted if there is no Confession. Only a priest may say the Absolution..

The Our Father may be said here, or later, on p. 16. It is used only once in MP and EP.

The Preces ("O Lord open thou our lips") on p. 7, with the Gloria Patri, is always used, except that the Gloria Patri may be omitted all through Holy Week.

The rubric which follows, on p. 8, allows for Psalm 95 to be used in place of the Venite, as printed on p. 9. As printed on p. 9, the final verses of Psalm 95 were deleted, and portions of Psalm 96 used as filler. In a revision of the 1928 BCP, it is likely that Psalm 95 will be used in its entirety, as it is in the 1662 BCP, because it has the word "today" in it…"today, if ye will hear my voice," *today* signifying this new day in the new creation.

The next rubric on p. 8 indicates that the Venite may be omitted on Ash Wednesday and Good Friday. As we shall see later, the Venite is supplanted on Thanksgiving Day by another psalm.

The antiphons on p. 8 are significant, for two reasons. It is intrinsically worthwhile to use antiphons with psalms and canticles, especially today, because they are "sound bites" in a time when people have short attention spans. They are also significant because they are the first time since 1549 that the loaded and theologically dense word "alleluia" comes back into the BCP. The Puritans insisted on getting rid of the word "alleluia." The word "alleluia" came back into the Liturgy through various hymnals, but not until 1928 in the Prayer Book, with our BCP and with Prayer Books coming out at that time in other countries. As for the Gradual and alleluia verses in the Mass, only in the Missals would "alleluia" be restored, but when the 1928 BCP is revised, the word "alleluia" will most certainly be in the Eucharistic Liturgy.

The reintroduction of "alleluia" in 1928 was tentative and gradualist, however, since the antiphon is only used at the beginning of the Venite. The normal way to use an antiphon is at the beginning **and end** of a psalm or canticle. The officiant reads, or chants, the beginning of the antiphon, up to the asterisk, then everyone joins in. Then the officiant reads, or chants, the beginning of the psalm or canticle, up to the asterisk, and then everyone joins in (everyone meaning sometimes those on his side of the aisle, in monastic use).

Regarding the rubric after the Venite, on p. 9: the Gloria Patri can be used in different ways. We use it after every psalm and canticle, and, in Psalm 119, after every section.

The final rubric on p. 9 provides the proper way to announce a reading at MP or EP: verse, chapter and book. "Here beginneth the ___ verse of the ___ chapter of Second Corinthians." At the end of the Lesson: Here endeth the (Second) Lesson."

Questions: regarding the 2nd rubric on p. 10 ("But note…") what significance do you see in this rubric? What would the Sunday morning Liturgy of the Word (what the PB calls the "Ante Communion") be like if we did it this way, compared with the way we all do it now? What is our source for the way we have the Liturgy of the Word in our Sunday Eucharist now (with an OT Lesson after the Collect, and a psalm or canticle after the OT Lesson)? (answer to this last part: the Reforms of Vatican II, which nearly everyone in the Western Church has followed).

Now let us dip back a little into the Psalms and Lessons for the Christian Year on p. x.

Every time you see a lesson in italics (always a First Lesson for MP or EP) it is from the Apocrypha. The Apocryphal books are those written between the Old and New Testaments. You will need to get a Bible that has the Apocrypha in it, and begin to familiarize yourself with its contents: apocalyptic books, historical books and wisdom literature.

Whenever you see an asterisk in front of a First Lesson for MP on Sundays, it means that lesson is especially thematically related to either the Epistle or the Gospel in the Eucharistic lectionary.

Note that every major feast begins with a vigil observance, Evening Prayer, the evening before. The first Evening Prayer is sometimes called First Evensong, every major feast having two Evening Propers. On p. xl, at the bottom, there is an Evening Prayer for Christmas Eve and one for Christmas Day. The evening of December 20 is the Vigil of St. Thomas, so on page xliv, in the column for Evening Prayer, there are propers for the "Eve," and for the day itself. This custom of a vigil service, of a feast beginning at sun-down the evening before, is of course taken from the synagogue and the sabbath observance. We begin in darkness, and move toward the light.

On pp. xlii–xliii are propers for special occasions for the Daily Offices. In the Missal, Masses for special occasions such as these listed here are called "Votive" Masses. The Prayer Book has a few "votive" Masses, on pp. 259-268. (On Thanksgiving Day, for example, propers for the Daily Offices would be on pp. xlii–xliii, and the Votive Mass for that day, on pp. 264-266).

Pages xliv–xlv show us the Psalms and Lessons for the Fixed Holy Days: the compilers of the 1789 BPB wanted to limit these days to those mentioned in the Bible, for simplicity in relating to non-liturgical Protestant bodies beginning to spread in the new country. The calendar on pp. xlvi–xlvii is quite spare. The 1662 BCP in England is much fuller, as are our Missals, put together in the 1930s and 40s. Our BCP has most of the "red letter days," meant always to be observed everywhere. "Black letter days" tend to be more local, or limited, observances.

**"Tables and Rules,"** pp. l & li:

The Church Year is based upon the date of Easter. When Easter comes early, Epiphanytide is compressed, and Trinitytide, lengthened. When Easter comes late, Epiphanytide is expanded, and Trinitytide, compressed.

A Table of Feasts indicate our minimum observances. A Table of Fasts is good to read through, to know it is here, to teach from. We tell people when to fast and abstain, but not how, although many dioceses have guidelines. We follow what is in the instruction section at the beginning of the *St. Augustine's Prayer Book.*

Tables of Precedence. You will use this frequently, to decide which days have priority, so that when St. Thomas (Dec 21) falls on a Sunday in Advent, you know that Sundays in Advent have precedence over everything else. But if St. Bartholomew (August 24) falls on a Sunday (which will be in Trinitytide) you will observe St. Bartholomew and commemorate whatever Sunday in Trinitytide is involved. A commemoration means that the propers for the dominant feast are used, and the observance being commemorated has its collect said, or sung, after that first one.

Question: if Easter comes very early, say, on March 24, and the Feast of the Annunciation (March 25) falls on Easter Monday (March 25), what feast do you observe on March 25, and when would you celebrate the Annunciation?

First rubric on p. 9–the Venite as printed on p. 10 is an adaptation of Psalm 95. It is permitted to use Psalm 95 as it stands in the Psalter. We do that at the Cathedral, as does the 1662 BCP, because Psalm 95 has the word "today" in it, which lends immediacy to an invitatory psalm. The 1789 revisers mistakenly thought that the ending of Psalm 95 was too grim for daily, or Sunday, use, so they chopped off the end and added parts of Psalm 96.

On Ash Wednesday and Good Friday, the Venite may be omitted. On Thanksgiving Day (p. 264) there is a substitution for it with the use of a portion of Psalm 147.

The Antiphons for the Venite were added in 1928. For the first time since 1552, the word "alleluia" comes back into the Liturgy of the BCP (the Puritans didn't like the use of that word). The antiphons are used at the beginning of the Venite only. Traditionally an antiphon is used at the beginning and end of a psalm or canticle.

Regarding the rubric at the bottom of p. 9: as noted above, the psalms can be selected four different ways–(i) using the psalm appointed in the lectionary (ii) using the "Daily Grind," the psalms for Day 1 (MP) and Day 1 (EP), by which method the psalms are read through once a month (iii) selecting a psalm from p. ix, for thematic reasons and (iv) minister's choice.

The last rubric on p. 9 indicates how the lessons are to be announced at the Daily Office (verse, chapter and book, with "Here beginneth the…verse of the…chapter of…," and "Here endeth the First (or Second) Lesson."

The T*e Deum* is good to use on Sundays, and feasts of our Lord, our Lady and the Apostles, and other major feast days. Otherwise, use the *Benedictus es*, on p. 11

The *Benedicite* on p. 11, a canticle calling on all creation to praise God, is good to use during Pre-Lent, beginning with Monday morning after Septuagesima Sunday, when the First Lesson is Genesis 1: 1-10, the beginning of creation. In the northern hemisphere things are starting to grow again, so the timing of the First Lesson and the use of this Canticle is not coincidental, but set up in the monasteries of the early Church.

The *Benedictus*, p. 14. This is the climax of MP. MP and EP, with the Gospel (Lucan) canticles, have the Incarnation as the filigree running through them. The dominant theme of the Eucharist, on the other hand, is the Paschal Mystery, Jesus' Death and Resurrection.

The weekdays are for the Incarnation, and Sunday is for the Resurrection. It is therefore best to use the *Benedictus* at MP.

There are a lot of musical settings for the canticles in the back of the Hymnal, in both Anglican Chant and Plainsong.

The Apostles' Creed on p. 15 is normally used. The reason the Nicene Creed is printed here is possibly because there have always been some parishes and missions which had very limited access to a priest, and so, seldom have the Eucharist. In order that they might be familiar with the Nicene Creed, its use is allowed in MP and EP.

The Our Father is used here, on p. 16, if not already said. The principle is that the Our Father is used at every service of the BCP.

p. 17–the Collect for the Day is said or sung here unless the Communion Service follows.

p. 17–the Collects for Peace and Grace follow.

The Litany may follow here, in which case MP ends with the Collects for Peace and Grace.

pp. 17–20: if the Litany is not read, any or all of these prayers may be used, ending with "The Grace" on p. 20.

Question, re, the prayer on p. 20. "Chrysostom" is a nickname. What was his first name? Where was he from, and where did he end up, and what writings is he famous for?

**Evening Prayer**

On p. 21, it is best to read only one sentence, using seasonal ones when appropriate.

p. 23, the long exhortation to confession is good for penitential seasons, and when there is plenty of time. Whenever a Mass follows the Daily Office, it is best to omit the General Confession here, since it will be said during the Mass.

p. 24, a lay reader will substitute a prayer for the Absolution, such as the Collect on p. 218. The Our Father can be said here, or after the Apostles' Creed.

p. 25, the Preces can be sung, using the music which is Hymn 601 in the Hymnal. The Ferial Preces are most commonly used; the Festal Preces (Hymn 602) usually imply the support of a choir.

p. 25, the Psalms come here. Remember the 4 ways of selecting Psalms—"the Daily Grind" (Day 1, MP & EP, Day 2, etc), the Lectionary, the Selection of Psalms (p. ix) and the Officiant's Choice. We do the Gloria Patri at the end of every Psalm, and, with Psalm 119, at the end of every section. In some places (including Orthodox Vespers) the Gloria in excelsis is said after the Psalms.

p. 26, the First Lesson, announced "Here beginneth the ___ verse of the ___ chapter of ___ (book). After the Lesson is said, "Here endeth the First Lesson."

p. 27, the Magnificat (Hymn tunes 647 to 658) is the climax of EP. It is almost always best to use the Magnificat.

p. 28, the Second Lesson, announced and concluded as above.

p. 28, the Nunc Dimittis (Hymn tunes 667–673). It is almost always best to use this Canticle.

p. 29, the Apostles' Creed, often chanted monotone (on one note)

p. 30, the Our Father, if it has not already been said. If the Creed was sung, so would be the Our Father, usually just on one note.

p. 31, the Suffrages after the Creed, Ferial and Festal, Hymns 601 and 602 (pp. 701–703).

p. 31, the Collect of the Day. If there is a saint's day or holy day, the Collect for the Day is said, or chanted first, and then the Collect for the previous Sunday.

p. 31, Collects for Peace & Grace. These are often chanted.

p. 31, "the Anthem," something sung by the choir, including sometimes the seasonal Marian antiphons, taken from the medieval liturgy, and now in manuals like the St. Augustine's PB.

p. 31, final rubric–what follows are prayers, rather than collects. They can all be used, or some, or none. Even if the collects were chanted, these prayers would not be. Each one is, in its own right, a theological, literary and aesthetic masterpiece. Massey Shepherd's PB Commentary gives some good and fascinating background on these prayers.

p. 34, we always conclude the Offices, and often, other devotions, with "the Grace," 2 Cor. 13.14. Hymns at EP could be placed at the beginning of the Office, after the Psalm(s), for an "Office Hymn," and after the Grace. If a sermon is preached at an Office, it could come after the hymn after the Grace, and could be followed by a final prayer and hymn.

**Prayers and Thanksgivings,** p. 35, the first four of these prayers are sometimes called, together with "A Prayer for the President…" on pp. 17 and 32, the "State Prayers." They were based on the prayers in the 1662 English BCP, but adapted for the 1789 BCP, after the United States won its independence from Great Britain. One can distill from them our theology and our understanding of the relationship between Church and State.

p. 38, "For those who are to be admitted into Holy Orders" Here are two prayers for "the Ember Days," the Wednesdays, Fridays and Saturdays in mid-December, then early in Lent, then in Whitsun-week, and then in mid–September, twelve days in all, when the Church tries to have its ordinations, with prayer and fasting for the ordinands. We also pray for seminaries and ministry and catechesis in general. We shall have occasion later to comment on the Ember Days. "Ember Days" is a nick name, possibly an Anglo-Saxon slurring of the French, *quatre temps*, four times, or four seasons. We can go down the rabbit hole of fascinating use, in the Family of God, of nicknames…Lent is a nickname, as is the word "Mass," and the word "Christmas," and "Easter," "Whitsunday," and later, we can highlight more nick-names.

p. 39, "For Fruitful Seasons," two fabulous prayers for Rogation Sunday and the Rogation Days. The Church was first with ecology. A full celebration of Rogationtide needs to be restored. The placement of Rogationtide, beginning with the Fifth Sunday after Easter, means that these four days occur just before Ascension Day. Our ultimate "rogating," or asking, is for the Holy Spirit, and Pentecost is nine days after Ascension. Lancelot Andrewes had something magnificent to say about the ascent of our flesh, in Christ, resulting in the descent of the Holy Spirit, in what he called "the Royal

Exchange." More can be said about this when we look at the Fifth Sunday after Easter, p. 175, and the Propers for the Rogation Days, p. 261.

p. 46, a note on all these prayers…they can be used in place of, or in addition to, the other prayers in MP and EP, after "the third Collect." They can also be used after the Nicene Creed at Mass, or even after the Post-communion prayer on p. 83.

"For a Person…going to Sea," this can be adapted by changing "the sea" to "the elements." and changing "the great deep" to "his way." "Dangers of the sea" can become "dangers of travel."

p. 47, "A Bidding Prayer." this was added in 1928. It can be used after the Nicene Creed at Mass, or in place of the prayers in MP and EP. It can also be used on Good Friday, in place of the Solemn Collects. It allows for the insertion of names, and at the end, it references the Communion of Saints.

p. 49, taken or adapted from various missals of the Western Church, for use as indicated in the rubric.

p. 50, to be used as indicated by the rubric.

**p. 54, the Litany**. there are two other litanies in the BCP, the Litany for the Dying, on p. 317, and the Litany for Ordinations, on p. 560. The question is often asked in our canonical exams,"how many litanies are in the BCP?" This Litany, the "Great Litany," came out a couple years before the 1549 BCP. Cranmer adapted it from the Latin Litany of the Saints, which is used in English on Easter Eve. The first breakthrough of English into the Liturgy came with the opening words of the Great Litany, "O God the Father, Creator of heaven and earth…" Those are the very first words of the Liturgy heard by Englishmen in their own tongue. The Litany can be sung in Procession all through Advent and Lent in place of the Opening Hymn, and can be used all through Advent and Lent, and indeed, at any time, as part of the Daily Offices. The Litany as a form is one of our deep liturgical connections with the Orthodox churches of the East, who use litanies more than collects.

p. 58, when we chant the Litany in Procession (on Sundays in Advent and Lent, in place of the Opening Hymn) we omit what follows after the Our Father, and skip down to the final prayer on p. 59. But if the Litany is used in a shorter service than the Eucharist, we would be more likely to say or sing the whole Litany.

p. 60, **A Penetential Office.** This is used on Ash Wednesday, followed by the Blessing and Imposition of Ashes (from the *Priest's Manual*, or from the Missal) followed by the Mass of the Day. This Service is sometimes used in parishes on Saturday evenings, after EP, as a preparation for Holy Communion (its placement right before the Eucharistic Liturgy is not coincidental). It is worth noting, in regard to the Unbound Ministry, that the word deliverance is used three times in this Office: once in Psalm 51, once in the Our Father, once at the top of p. 92. Another word like deliver, "loose," is used on p. 63.

# THE HOLY COMMUNION AND THE COLLECTS, EPISTLES, AND GOSPELS

p. 65, the title page for the Holy Communion, begins a new section which in the Middle Ages was a book called "The Missal," of everything pertaining to the Eucharist.

p. 67, in many places the Decalogue is said, with sung or said responses, on the first Sunday of the month. Some parishes do not use the Decalogue. Other parishes do the Decalogue, the Summary of the Law on p. 69, the Kyrie on p. 70 and the Collect following it on p. 70. In that case the Gloria in excelsis goes at the end of the Liturgy, on p. 83. The rubric on the bottom of p. 67 gives the various ways we can configure Cranmer's Penitential Rite, which picks up on the Lutheran paradigm of Law, then Gospel.

pp. 68–69, The responses to the Decalogue can be chanted, using the Merbecke setting in the Hymnal, #701, or other settings.

p. 70, the Kyrie can be 3 fold or 9 fold, chanted or said. In most of our parishes we follow the Kyrie with the Gloria in Excelsis, which is a doxology to the Kyrie. In some parishes, the Gloria goes after the Post communion Thanksgiving, on

p. 83, which is where Cranmer put it from 1552 onwards. It is perfectly alright in either place. In the Liturgy of St. John Chrysostom, there is no Gloria in excelsis. The Orthodox use it only at Vespers.

p. 70, the first salutation ("The Lord be with you") is the beginning of the Liturgy of the Word.

The Collect of the Day may be followed by the Collect of an Octave, or (on a weekday) the Collect of the preceding Sunday, or the Collect for a season, such as Advent or Lent. Some Sundays are simple, as on the Second Sunday after the Epiphany, p. 111, when there is only one Collect.

The Epistle is announced chapter, book and verse. "The Epistle is written in the 12th chapter of Romans, beginning at the 6th verse." At the end of the Epistle, the minister says "Here endeth the Epistle," and we add "Thanks be to God." There are other ways to announce the Epistle, but it is good to have one set way in a parish, and the Prayer Book way is best because everyone has a copy of the Prayer Book and can follow it. Why Cranmer has a way of announcing lessons for the Daily Offices that is different from the Eucharist is open to speculation.

A note on the words "minister" and "priest" in the rubrics: "Priest" means someone ordained to that Office, and what is indicated in the rubric is that only a priest or someone "higher up" can do what is indicated. "Minister" refers to someone who could be "lower" than a priest, eg, a deacon or sub-deacon or lay reader or head of a household.

On p. 70 is a rubric allowing a Hymn or an Anthem after the Epistle. The hymn could be a psalm, of course. Having a hymn, psalm or anthem here can allow for a Gospel Procession. In the Missal, the Gradual and Alleluia verse would be chanted or said here (alleluia being omitted in Pre Lent and Lent). "Gradual" comes from the Latin word for grade, or step, and as we process out from the Altar and return to it, we are going up and down the steps, or grades.

p. 70, We stand for the Gospel, to show our readiness to follow Christ. If there is a Deacon, he sings or says the Gospel. Torches and incense are used here whenever possible. The Sub deacon holds the book for the Deacon. The Deacon announces the Gospel, chapter, book and verse. "The Holy Gospel is written in the 24th chapter of St. Luke, beginning at the 49th verse." Everyone says or sings "Glory be to thee, O Lord," and the Deacon censes the Gospel Book with three single swings, center, left and right. After the Gospel, everyone says or sings, "Praise be to thee, O Christ." The Sub deacon takes the Gospel Book and leads the Gospel procession back to the Altar, the Deacon going last. The Sub deacon presents the Gospel book to the Celebrant, who kisses it, and the Celebrant is censed. This ceremonial shows the singing or reading of the Gospel for the Day as a solemn Proclamation, above and beyond a reading, the light and love of Christ, the eternal Gospel, coming to each of us, and to the world, directly.

p. 71, the Nicene Creed (for Sundays and all Feasts of Our Lord and of Our Lady and Apostles and Doctors of the Church) In some places the Athanasian Creed is used on Trinity Sunday. In the Church of England, if the 1662 BCP is being followed, the Athanasian Creed is also used on all feasts of Apostles. The Nicene Creed is our response to the Gospel. In many places we geneflect at the *Incarnatus*, the words "And was incarnate by the Holy Ghost of the Virgin

Mary, and was made man." In some churches the word "holy," deleted by accident by a scribe, is put back in so as to read "And I believe in one holy Catholic and Apostolic Church..." The sign of the Cross is made at the end, the Cross being our gateway to eternal Life.

Question: using only the BCP: it is December 14, Ember Wednesday in Advent. What are the 3 collects that could be used, and in what order? (for brevity, or for pastoral reasons you might want to use only the first, or the first two collects).

Super tricky trivia question — if using the Missal as well as the PB (in the Missal, not only is Dec 14 an Ember Day...it is also a weekday following Advent 3, and it is in the Season of Advent, and it is in the Octave of the Conception of the Blessed Virgin Mary) so there are 4 collects that could be used...which ones, and in which order? The order for the last 2 collects is negotiable. Again, in real life, for brevity's sake, or for other pastoral reasons, you might want to use only the first one, or the first two, or three.

Hint–The BCP is unique among liturgies of the universal Church in having two seasonal collects (a collect which is to be read every day during the season) and these are the seasonal Collect for Advent, on p. 90, and the seasonal Collect for Lent, on p. 124, with rubrics for their use.

p. 71, the first rubric covers announcements, possible "family time" (special intercessions, a church school skit, presentation of layreaders' licenses, reception of new vestry members, or altar guild members, or ACW members, etc.)

p. 71, the second rubric–special intercessions, especially pertaining to the parish family, are possible here. Note how the Bidding Prayer may be said here (p. 47). The Bidding Prayer was written in 1928, and allowed here in 1928, to begin to see the effect of having all the intercessions here, as in the Rites of the 1979 Book, and in all the post Vatican II rites of the Western Church.

p. 71, third rubric–the Sermon is actually mandatory, although it is sometimes shortened to a homily, or omitted at a Low Mass. On p. 72–73, we begin the Offertory, with the Offertory Sentences. One of these is sufficient, and can be selected thematically. We see in the second rubric on p. 73 the Deacon's role in the Offertory. The third rubric was/is controversial among Calvinists: for a priest to make an offering of bread and wine is the beginning of a sacrifice and reveals the fact that the Eucharist is a sacrifice–not to repeat Christ's once-for-all Sacrifice, but to make *anamnesis* of it…to re-present it…to make it effectual in the lives of the worshippers, *to perform the mercy*. In the Missal the element of sacrifice is made even more explicit when the priest says, at the end of the Offertory, "Pray, brethren, that this my sacrifice and yours…"

p. 73, the priest, or the deacon, may "bid the prayers of the people," making mention of specific sick folks or special needs, naming those in ecclesiastical and civil authority, those serving in the Armed Forces, etc. Praying for "the whole state" of Christ's Church was/is controversial among Calvinists, since the "whole state" means the living and the departed, and strict Calvinists do not pray for the departed. This prayer is part of the Offertory, and replaces the old medieval "secret" (a prayer said secretly by the priest toward the end of the Offertory). We ask that our alms and oblations (bread and wine) be received by God, along with our prayers. In Cranmer's 1549 Book this Prayer was part of the Canon of

Consecration, just as it was part of the old Gregorian Canon. It was separated out in 1552, and has been separate ever since. In 1928, under the final section for the departed, the phrase "grant them continual growth in thy love and service" was added. It is the first time since 1549 that we pray directly for the departed. Prayer for the departed (here and elsewhere) was one of the biggest (and to some extent most controversial) revisions made in 1928, as we shall see further on.

p. 75, if there is to be an Exhortation, it would come after the Prayer for the Church. Many parishes follow the rubric and use the Exhortation, usually the short one on p. 85, on the First Sunday in Advent, the First Sunday in Lent, and Trinity Sunday. The Congregation may stand for it. There is a lot of Eucharistic theology in the Exhortations. More on that later.

pp. 75–76, the short Exhortation ("Ye who do truly..."), the General Confession, the Absolution and the Comfortable Words, form a section which could be called "Communion Devotions," or preparation for Holy Communion. In 1549 this section was immediately preceding Communion. In many post Vatican II liturgies, it is put at the very beginning of the Liturgy of the Word. It is appropriate here, as part of the Offertory, offering bread, wine, alms, intercessions, and now, our sins, just before the great Sursum Corda.

p. 76, it would seem that Cranmer got the idea for "Comfortable Words" that follow the Absolution from Luther, who did this sort of thing. The Orthodox, in the Liturgy of St. John Chrysostom, insert portions of Scripture such as the Beatitudes, into the liturgical narrative.

Question: what other Lutheran influence(s) do you find in our Eucharistic Liturgy in its current form, the 1928 BCP?

(hint–think of the Law–Gospel paradigm, and where that appears in a portion of our Liturgy. There are other influences too, involving "justification by faith," the starting point for Lutheran systematic theology. Our starting point is the Incarnation, as with the Fathers of the first eight centuries.

p. 76, the Sursum Corda, "Lift up your hearts," the beginning of the Eucharistic Prayer, also known as the Great Thanksgiving, or the Canon of Consecration.

p. 77, Proper Prefaces. These are said on the day indicated, and when said on the day plus seven other days, they form part of the observance of "the Octave," the after-glow of the feast. The Feast of the Transfiguration was added in 1892. The days that have octaves are Christmas, Epiphany, Easter, Ascension, Whitsunday and All Saints' Day.

The Missal (both American and Anglican) has more days with octaves: Conception of the BVM, St. Stephen, Holy Innocents, St. John, Corpus Christi, Sacred Heart and Assumption of the Blessed Virgin Mary, plus some others.

The Missal makes the assumption that most Masses should have a proper preface. So, for example, in Trinitytide, one of the proper prefaces for Trinity Sunday is used every Sunday. Ferias in Trinitytide do not have a proper preface, and although some saints' days do, there are some that do not. A feria, by the way, is a day not celebrating anyone or anything in particular. It is neither a feast day nor a fast day.

p. 80, the American Canon. This was put into the 1789 American BCP by Bishop Samuel Seabury as a condition set by the Scottish Episcopal Church for his consecration. The most significant things added to the old 1662 Canon are (i) "the Oblation," or *anamnesis*–the re-presentation of Jesus' passion, death, resurrection and ascension, such that these saving events are immediately available and present to the worshippers, and (ii) "the Invocation," or *epiclesis*, the invocation of the Holy Spirit. This restoration of the *epiclesis* is very significant in the life of the Church. For centuries it dropped out of most western eucharistic liturgies, and is now restored by our English speaking community, to help reveal the fact that everything in the Kingdom is *epicletic*; everything is in the Holy Spirit...*in the Spirit, through the Son, to the Father.*

Our Canon reinforces the Catholic doctrine of Eucharistic sacrifice ... the the Mass is a sacrifice ... by citing (i) Jesus perfect sacrifice (ii) our re-presentation of that sacrifice through our offering of the bread and wine, which are now "these holy gifts," (iii) "our sacrifice of praise and thanksgiving" and (iv) our sacrifice of ourselves. So the Eucharistic Sacrifice is (i) Jesus' Sacrifice, (ii) the Church's Sacrifice, and (iii) the worshipper's sacrifice. The Our Father on p. 82 concludes the Canon.

In most of our parishes the Fraction takes place here, and if the Missal is used there is a prayer (the *Libera Nos*) which the celebrant says privately while he breaks the Host. In Cranmer's Liturgy the Host is broken just before the words of institution, as indicated in the rubric on p. 80. His is the only Liturgy where the Bread is broken at that point.

The Commixture: in the Missal, after the Host is broken, a second, smaller break is made, and a particle of the Host is put into the Chalice while the celebrant says "The Peace of the Lord be alway with you," our Lord's words to the apostles after the Resurrection. The Commixture symbolizes the Resurrection, the reuniting of Jesus' Body and Blood.

In the Missal, the Agnus Dei is said or sung at this point, and then comes the Prayer of Humble Access. In the PB, the Agnus Dei comes after the Prayer of Humble Access. The Agnus Dei was widely added back into our Liturgy with the 1940 Hymnal, which has various musical settings for it. The 1928 Book allows for it with a rubric, "Here may be sung a hymn." It was controversial among Calvinists, who objected to saying "O Lamb of God" with the consecrated elements on the Altar, lest they be thought "sacramental realists," ie, the Bread and Wine are the real presence of the Lamb of God; they *are* the very Lamb of God, which, of course, we believe.

p. 83, the Ablutions–the PB rubric has them after the Service is over. In the 19th century, one of the influences of the Oxford/Tractarian/Ritualist Movements is that we used the Continental Roman model for upgrading our ceremonial, and, out of greater reverence for the Sacrament, we consume what is left and cleanse the vessels immediately after Communion.

On p. 83 is Cranmer's Post-communion thanksgiving, a theological and aesthetic masterpiece. The Eucharistic theology here is very patristic. There was once an atheistic professor of English in a Canadian university who taught this to his class as the most elegant prose ever composed in the entire history of our English language. (The complete story of this English professor is found in Robertson Davies's *The Rebel Angels*)

Question: can you identify some of the patristic word couplets and longer patristic phraseology in Cranmer's Post communion thanksgiving?

p. 84, the Gloria in excelsis–this is omitted in Advent, Pre-Lent and Lent. In the patristic period this entered the Liturgy as a doxology to the Kyrie Eleison, and that is its place in the Missals we use, and in Cranmer's 1549 Prayer Book. It was, by 1552, put at the end of the Liturgy, where it appears in our 1928 Prayer Book today. Cranmer may have had more than one reason for putting it there: he wanted the act of receiving Holy Communion to be in the middle of the Rite, with as much following Communion as preceding, to reveal the reception of Communion (so neglected in medieval times) as central and climactic.

Another reason is that if there is a Short Morning Prayer to begin the Liturgy (as per the rubric on p. 10), the MP part of the Liturgy would end with a Te Deum (p. 10) as a hymn for moving to the Altar. Cranmer loved balance, and to have a Te Deum followed so closely by the Gloria, nearly back-to-back, meant that the Gloria should go at the end. It is perhaps the case that about one quarter of parishes using the '28 Book have the Gloria in excelsis at the end.

"General Rubrics"–the first one indicates what a Deacon may do (the 3 things a Deacon may not do are to bless, consecrate and absolve). We extrapolate from this rubric the "Deacon's Mass," which should really be called a Pre-Sanctified Liturgy. The Deacon does the whole Communion Service, omitting the Absolution, the Sursum Corda, the Prayer of Consecration and the Blessing at the end (substituting perhaps the final prayer on p. 63, sometimes called the "Aaronic Blessing.") The Deacon celebrating a Pre-Sanctified Liturgy administers the Body of Christ from the Tabernacle.

The second rubric refers to what was often called the "Ante-Communion," and is now more often called "the Liturgy of the Word."

The third rubric refers to the Ablutions, which, since the Tractarian/Ritualist movement in the 19th and 20th centuries, have been done right after everyone receives Communion, more in keeping with the practice of the universal Church, and less likely to result in neglect or abuse.

The fourth and fifth rubrics pertain to Communion discipline and excommunication. A man openly committing adultery, for example, must not come for the Sacrament, until he repents and amends his life. The Minister must report anyone excommunicated to the Bishop within 14 days.

p. 85, the Exhortations—one of these is to be read after the Prayer for the Church on the First Sunday in Advent, the First Sunday in Lent, and Trinity Sunday. Most parishes use the first one, the short one. All three have very sound teaching on the Eucharist, and the Christian's responsibilities in relation to it. The second Exhortation, on p. 88, is the first place in the PB that refers specifically to sacramental Confession: "if there be any of you, who by this means cannot quiet his own conscience…let him come to me…"

It is good to know that the 1928 BCP makes 3 specific references to Sacramental Confession: (i) the second Exhortation on p. 88, (ii) the Visitation of the Sick, in the second rubric on p. 313 (and what follows that rubric, on the bottom of p. 313 and all of p. 314 is almost or could be an Absolution, and (iii) on p. 546, in the Ordering of Priests, when the Bishop says the Ordination Prayer, "Whose sins thou dost forgive…" quoting from John 20:23.

There is an old saying among Anglicans regarding the Sacrament of Confession: "all may, some should, none must." But to really fall in love with God, to correspond dynamically with His graces and to let Him "perform the mercy" in our lives, we are going to want earnestly to go to Confession and receive the inestimable benefits of Absolution. The priest (himself a penitent) will want to teach, and preach, frequently and with enthusiasm, how we discover, in this Sacrament, what our Baptisms mean. The Sacrament of Confession is related to Baptism, in that the Holy Spirit restores, in Absolution, our baptismal union with Christ.

We can work toward increasing the number of penitents in our parishes by teaching and preaching the significance of the Sacrament of Absolution, and, also, by requiring it of adults preparing for baptism, and of adults and young people preparing for confirmation. At the St. Michael's Conference, everyone is encouraged to go to confession during the week, and participation is effectively 100%. The seven Sacraments are all of a piece in the Church, the Church being the Sacrament of the Holy Spirit. Thus, our life in Christ is

initiated in Baptism
sealed in Confirmation
restored in Confession/Absolution
nourished in Holy Communion
revealed in Holy Matrimony
healed in Holy Unction
enabled in Holy Orders
Question: what is/are your favorite title(s)
for the Eucharist, and why?

# THE COLLECTS, EPISTLES AND GOSPELS

To be used throughout the Year

p. 90, We see in our collects and other prayers the old Anglican rule of thumb, "lex orandi, lex credendi," the law of prayer is the law of belief. Our beliefs, our theology, as Anglicans, is to a large extent summed up in the prayers of our Liturgy.

The 1st rubric on p. 90: as daily Eucharists became more common throughout the Church, this was put in to cover weekdays that are not "red letter" saints days.

The 2nd rubric: the first Evening Prayer of a Sunday or a feast day is the evening before, or the vigil, and the collect for the next day may be read. So at Evening Prayer on Saturday you would read the Collect for the Sunday following, or on the evening before the Feast of St. Matthias, February 24, you would read the Collect for St. Matthias Day, plus the Collect for the previous Sunday, followed by the Collect for Lent.

The Collect for Advent Sunday is also seasonal (to be read every day throughout Advent, after the Collect of the Day)

In parishes which have an Old Testament lesson after the Collect, we select these from p. x and following. The Old Testament lesson for MP that has an asterisk is thematically suited for the Epistle and Gospel. The psalms chosen for a given Sunday or feast are also thematically appropriate for the other propers.

Cranmer eliminated most of the "Minor Propers" even in 1549, keeping only vestiges of them. Luther kept them all. The Minor Propers are the Introit, the Gradual, the Offertory verse and the Communion verse. The missals put together by Anglicans in the mid-twentieth century restored the Minor Propers. There, every Mass has an Introit, a Gradual and alleluia verse (or a tract, in Lent), an Offertory verse and a Communion verse. In patristic times these verses would have been entire psalms.

With the use of hymns, which began to be compiled and used in the 17–18th century and later, we often substitute a hymn for an introit psalm, or the gradual, etc.

There are various styles of collects, and different times of their compositions. The Collect for Advent 1 is Cranmer's paraphrase of an old medieval collect. The Collect for Advent 2 is completely drafted by Cranmer from scratch, to create a new reformation theme for Advent 2, "Bible Sunday."

p. 96, the Christmas Day Collect is to be said daily throughout the Octave. Christmas is a Feast that has an Octave.

p. 108, the rubric indicates that Epiphany is also a Feast that has an Octave.

p. 112, notice how short this Collect is. Very short Collects are from the times when Rome was falling (5th–6th centuries) and people were subject to violence, chaos, hunger and plague.

p. 117, this Collect is quite long. Long collects were generally composed in the 17th century, not by Cranmer. They reflect the theology of the "Caroline Divines." Long collects and exhortations (as on pp. 85-89) show an awareness of a newly literate society in which people can take on large chunks of written material and exult in their ability to do so.

In the Middle Ages, when few could read, we have lots of sound bites (sentences and phrases of Scripture) and by the 16th–17th centuries, England has become a highly literate society with a very learned clergy and, eventually, an emerging strong tradition of lay theologians.

Question–do you prefer the sound bite method of teaching and preaching, or the presentation of larger portions of Scripture, or both?

"Extra credit"–who were some of the "Caroline Divines," and do you have any favorites among them?

Hint: in his book, *Restoring the Anglican Mind*, Arthur Middleton names most of them. If you Google "Caroline Divines" a quite respectable article on this comes up.

p. 124, The Collect for Ash Wednesday is seasonal, used throughout the Season of Lent, after the Collect of the Day.

p. 125, This rubric says that a day which has no propers of its own uses the propers from the previous Sunday.

p. 132, On Passion Sunday, in many churches, the crosses in the church are veiled in violet (when practicable), as are statues and icons.

p. 134, The Collect for Palm Sunday is used after the Collect of the Day, every day until Good Friday.

The Gospel for Palm Sunday is, in the Missal, "the Passion of our Lord Jesus Christ according to Matthew." (the Gospel for the Day is read before the Mass, as part of the Blessing of the Palms). "The Passion" is announced by a lector, as indicated above, with no "Glory be to thee, O Lord before, and no "Praise be to thee, O Christ," after. The people, or a choir, may read, or chant, the parts belonging to the Crowd, or to others who are speaking. The Celebrant may read the parts spoken by Christ.

p. 138, On Monday before Easter we begin "The Passion of our Lord Jesus Christ, according to Mark."

p. 144, On Tuesday before Easter we continue "The Passion of our Lord Jesus Christ, according to Mark."

p. 148, On Wednesday before Easter we begin "The Passion of our Lord Jesus Christ, according to Luke."

p. 152, On Maundy Thursday we finish "the Passion of our Lord Jesus Christ, according to Luke," or, p. 155, use the account of the foot washing in John's Gospel. "Maundy" is a nick-name for the Latin, "mandatum," or commandment, on this day when our Lord gives us the commandment "to love one another."

p. 156, Traditionally, no Mass is celebrated today, and so Holy Communion is received from the Reserved Sacrament. Today we have "The Passion of our Lord Jesus Christ, according to John."

p. 161, Traditionally, no Mass is celebrated today. In parishes using the Missal, the propers on p. 161 can be used for a Vigil Mass. Or the Vigil of Easter can be celebrated in its entirety from one of the Missals. This Vigil begins as the sun is setting, or after, with the Blessing of the New Fire, the Blessing of the Paschal Candle with the Exsultet, the Prophecies, the Blessing of the Font (possibly with Baptisms), the Litany of the Saints, and the first Mass of Easter.

p. 162, The Easter Anthem, paraphrased from I Cor. 15, is used at MP in place of the Venite, throughout the Octave of Easter. In some places, the Easter Anthem is sung after the Opening Hymn on Easter morning. There is music for it in the Hymnal, 680–683.

p. 163, Since Easter has an Octave, this Collect is used every day in the Octave, after the Collect of the Day.

p. 165, Here is a second set of propers for Easter Day. Traditionally, this second set of propers is used "at the first Communion," eg, the Vigil Mass of Easter, the evening before, or, at an early Mass on Easter morning. The first set is used at the main Mass of Easter morning.

p. 166, The PB has propers for Easter Monday and Easter Tuesday. The Missal has propers for all 6 weekdays after Easter Day. The Easter week post communions in the *Anglican Missal* are magnificent.

p. 177, Easter lasts, in our customary, 40 days, and ends the evening before Ascension Day. So at the Ascension Day Mass, after the Gospel, we extinguish the Paschal Candle.

Easter is the center of the Church Year. Every movable feast is based on the date of Easter. Easter is the Queen of Seasons because the Resurrection is the heart of the Christian Faith; the Resurrection *is* the Gospel.

Question: We highlight the significance of Easter by basing the Church Year on the date of Easter. Can you think of some things we do, or have, liturgically, that highlight this Season…that highlight the Resurrection? (hint–one such thing is mentioned above, under "p. 177." Another is in the middle of p. 278. There are more!)

p. 175, "Rogation Sunday." We begin the little season of Rogationtide. "Rogation" comes from the Latin word, "rogare," to ask, and during this season we ask for God's blessing on the crops that are being planted in our part of the world, and for good stewardship of all resources: livestock, forests, fisheries, coal mines, oil wells, business, commerce, transport and trade. The ultimate thing we ask for is the Giver of these gifts, for the gift of the Holy Spirit. Rogation tide ends with Ascension Day, and the ascent of our flesh in Christ means the descent of His Spirit, in what Lancelot Andrewes called a "Royal Exchange." Here is an example of his brilliant theological mind, so steeped in the Eastern fathers.

The Propers on p. 175 set the stage for Rogationtide, naming God in the Collect as the author of all good things, and in the Epistle, citing the visitation of the fatherless and widows as part of our stewardship of creation, and in the Gospel, hearing Jesus' teaching about asking.

In some parishes, especially in old England, there would be a Rogation Sunday procession before Mass, to process to a place where a tree would be planted, or a bush, or where a garden or some crops or livestock would be blessed. The procession then might walk the entire parish's boundaries, or a portion of them, while singing hymns (since parishes in England all have specific boundaries), claiming everyone and everything in the boundaries for the Kingdom. This procession has been nicknamed "Beating the Bounds," since the choirboys in the procession would carry sticks, and whack them at the boundary line as they go forward.

The color for Rogation Sunday is white.

The Monday, Tuesday and Wednesday after Rogation Sunday are the "Rogation Days." We fast and pray on these days, and the color is violet. The Propers are on pp. 261-262, and we pray for a fruitful season, and hear from Ezekiel about the blessings of God's covenant of peace, and in the Gospel are pointed by our Lord towards the Holy Spirit, the ultimate gift.

During the Daily Offices on these days we can use the prayers on pp. 39-40, "For Fruitful Seasons." Each of these prayers gives us a theological matrix for what would later be called "ecology." We can see with Rogationtide that the Church was first in ecology, and that we have the resources in our Liturgy for a complete theology of creation, and stewardship of it. The earth is not our mother, but, as Francis of Assisi would say, our sister. Our Mother is a person, Mary. The earth, and all creation, which is styled as feminine before God, is our sister. This is important teaching for today, when so many outside the Church are looking for a "green" spirituality.

It is also fitting on the Rogation Days to use the Litany, either with the Daily Offices, or with the Eucharist.

p. 177, Ascension Day, beginning the nine day novena, or nine day preparation, for Pentecost. Ascension Day has an Octave, so the Collect for the Day is repeated daily for the Feast plus seven days. So on the Sunday after Ascension Day, you would read the Collect for that day, on p. 179, plus the one for Ascension Day. Also, Ascension Day has a proper preface just before the Sanctus. On Ascension Day, after the Gospel is sung, or read, the Paschal Candle is extinguished, and, after the Liturgy, returned to its place next to the Font.

Father Alexander Schmemann, in his masterpiece, *The Eucharist, Sacrament of the Kingdom*, describes the Eucharist as the Sacrament of our Ascension in Christ. In the Spirit, we ascend with Christ to the heavenlies, to worship before the Throne in the glory of the new creation. We are lifted up in the Sursum Corda, and when we sing the Sanctus, we are hearing and seeing Heaven.

There are two perspectives, two sides of the same coin, about the Eucharistic presence. In the West, we tend toward the view that "God comes down onto this Altar." In the Eastern Church, there is a tendency to see how "we are lifted up, in the Spirit, to the heavenlies."

Question: can you locate, in Ephesians and Colossians, the texts that lie behind this perspective of Father Schmemann's?

p. 180, Whitsunday has an Octave, and the Collect for Whitsunday is used every day in it, after any Collect for the Day. There are two sets of propers for Whitsunday. Whitsunday is a nick-name (there are many nick-names in the Family of God, such as "Lent," and "Mass," and "Christmas" and "Ember Day.")

Whitsunday can either refer to "White Sunday" when the color for the day would have been white, or, as is more likely, to the old Anglo-Saxon word "wit," which means "wits," or "knowledge," or "wisdom." ("wit" dom), a gift of the Holy Spirit.

pp. 183–186, Monday and Tuesday after Whitsunday were added in 1928. A revision of 1928 would almost certainly add Wednesday through Saturday in Whitsun Week, and this is what the Missal has. Of course, in a way, the 1928 BCP already has Wednesday in Whitsun Week, and Friday and Saturday, because of the Ember Days in Whitsun Week, Wednesday, Friday and Saturday, which have propers on p. 260.

We will speak more of Ember Days when we get to p. 260.

p. 186, Trinity Sunday is the "Feast of Orthodoxy." The long season of Trinity is shortened if Easter comes late, and is lengthened if Easter comes early. After the Reformation, the countries of Northern Europe kept Trinitytide as a season. South of the Alps, the tradition was, as it is in post Vatican II reforms, to have a long season of Sundays after Pentecost.

Trinity Sunday is the full revelation of the triune God, the God who is love: Lover, Beloved, and the Love between them, Personified. Fr. Schmemann used to say that the Kingdom is (or subsists in) the love of the Father for the Son, and the love of the Son for the Father, and the Holy Spirit's gift of that Love for the faithful.

On the Sundays after Trinity, we begin to unpack some of what this inexpressible gift of love is:

Trinity 1: "love one another." "take care of Lazarus, who is at your doorstep."

Trinity 2: "we love the brethren." The call to our Lord's Supper is unconditional, the Supper which is (again quoting Fr. Schmemann) "the gift of the goal…where all is fulfilled, all is granted."

Trinity 3: "the God of all grace…" "this man receiveth sinners…" This is our only hope…He looks for us sinners until He finds us.

Trinity 4: "the whole creation is standing on tip-toe to see the sons of God coming into their own." The Gospel from Luke is the Sermon on the Plain. "forgive, and ye shall be forgiven…give, and it shall be given unto you…"

Trinity 5: "be ye all of one mind, having compassion one of another…" "Launch out into the deep…Let down your nets for a draught…" We seek to bring all men into the Kingdom of the Father's love for the Son, and the Son's love for the Father, and the Holy Spirit's gift of that love for all men.

Question: Do you prefer to have Sundays after Trinity, or Sundays after Pentecost? (there is no one correct answer to this). Why do you have this preference? What might be some of the different theological emphases in each of these approaches? Does one or the other seem more profound to you?

(It is perfectly alright to believe that they are equal in value, but that each one does have its own way of seeing life in the Kingdom. Can you nuance that?)

p. 224, the rubric at the bottom: if Trinitytide is long (when Easter comes early), Sundays after Epiphany are used. The Sunday next before Advent, p. 225, is always used. Epiphany tide and Trinitytide are accordion-like, depending on an early or a late Easter.

In most of the Western Church since Vatican II, the final Sunday in Trinitytide (or Pentecost, or "Ordinary Time") is the Feast of Christ the King. But nearly all '28 BCP parishes that observe the Feast of Christ the King do so in the old time slot, the last Sunday in October.

p. 225, When an Old Testament lesson serves as the Epistle, it can be announced this way: "That portion of Holy Scripture designated as the Epistle is written in the 23rd chapter of Jeremiah, beginning at the 5th verse." At the end: "Here endeth the Lesson." I have sometimes used: "The Epistle is taken from the 23rd chapter of Jeremiah, beginning at the 5th verse."

p. 226, This section is the Proper of Saints. It begins with St. Andrew, because his feast day is the first in the new Church Year that begins with Advent I in late November or early December.

p. 247, The Feast of the Transfiguration: this was added to the PB as a red letter feast in 1892, with a Proper Preface on p. 77. The Transfiguration of our Lord is for the Orthodox the paradigm for life in the Kingdom.

p. 256, All Saints' Day. As per the rubric, this Feast has an Octave (the Collect is read on the Feast Day plus seven more, after whatever Collect there may be for a day. All Saints also has a Proper Preface on p. 79.

p. 258, A Saint's Day: this was added in 1928, because daily Masses were becoming more common, and these propers can cover any saint who is not in the foregoing Proper.

p. 259–268, This begins a section which in the Missal would be called the Votive Masses (Masses for particular occasions or causes). The Missals have many more votive Masses than the PB.

pp. 268–269, The Burial of the Dead. This Proper, added in 1928, is a special kind of votive Mass called in the Missal a "Requiem Mass," or "Mass for the Dead." Prayer for the dead, added in 1928, was somewhat controversial at the time. It was the most significant revision of the '28 Book.

pp. 271–342, This begins a new section, **the Pastoral Offices**, which go in order from birth to death.

# THE MINISTRATION OF HOLY BAPTISM

*together with*
The Offices of Instruction
The Order of Confirmation
The Solemnization of Matrimony
The Thanksgiving after Child-birth
The Visitation of the Sick
The Communion of the Sick
The Burial of the Dead

p. 273, Note the rubric on godparents.

p. 273–274, Question: based on the exhortation that begins on p. 273 and the prayer on p. 274, what is the inward and spiritual meaning of Holy Baptism (the outward sign being baptism with water in the Name of the Trinity)

Addional questions: On pp. 274–275, each of the three Gospel readings begins with an announcement of the reading, citing the Gospel, the chapter and the verse, in that order. At Mass, the Epistle and Gospel are announced differently (cf. p. 70): chapter, book, and verse.

How is a Lesson at MP or EP to be announced (broad hint–the answer is on p. 9 at the bottom)? How is it to be concluded?

Question for which no one knows the answer: Why are lessons at MP and EP announced one way, and the Epistles at Mass announced another?

One possible theory: Cranmer did this to create a difference between the Daily Office and the Mass. The difference is aesthetic.

In announcing an Old Testament reading at Mass (for which there is no provision in the '28 BCP) these forms may be used: "A Reading from Isaiah," or, "A Reading from the Book of the Prophet Isaiah," or, "A Reading from Isaiah, chapter 12."

In announcing Epistles and Gospels, the word "book" is not used, but "Epistle," and "Gospel." So for example, one does not say "the Book of Romans," but "the Epistle to the Romans." One does not say, "the Book of Mark," but "the Gospel according to Mark (or St. Mark)."

BCP. p. 268–these propers for a Requiem Mass were added in 1928. For the first time since 1549, we pray in the Liturgy for the dead. This was somewhat controversial in 1928.

pp. 273–282–as opportunity allows, look in the *Priests' Manual* to see what ceremonies are added to the BCP Liturgy (using blessed salt, and the Oil of the Catechumens, and the Chrism, and a candle lit from the Paschal Candle) Laymen, or those who do not have a *Priests" Manual,* just go on to p. 280 below)

p. 280–the rubric at the top, "Here the Minister shall make a Cross upon the Child's forehead," is the one time the BCP mentions the sign of the cross. 1662 kept it, even though the Puritans wanted it taken out.

p. 281–the rubric in the middle–the order we follow is Baptism, Confirmation and then admission to Holy Communion. The Orthodox also follow this order, but do everything at once at the Baptism. The Romans admit to Communion before Confirmation.

pp. 281–282, Notice the sections on Private Baptism, Receiving of One Privately Baptized, and Conditional Baptism.

pp. 283–295, **The Offices of Instruction** were introduced in the 1928 BCP as a part of the Liturgy. Each Office could be used in place of a sermon. The First Office is taken from the old Catechism (pp. 577-583). The Second Office (pp. 290–295) has new material in it about the Church and the Ministry. Both Offices are excellent preparation for Confirmation.

p. 295, In the rubrics here the Minister is responsible for the catechism of his people, young and old. He may delegate this, but he is ultimately responsible, and should take an active part in catechesis. The final rubric provides what is required for Confirmation.

pp. 296–299, Here is **The Order of Confirmation**. On p. 297, after the Confirming Prayer, the confirmand is anointed with Chrism. This anointing is not in the Prayer Book, but would almost certainly be put into a revision. The Chrism for anointing (consecrated olive oil and balsalm) is the same used in the anointing of: (i) the newly baptized, (ii) a newly ordained priest's hands, (iii) a chalice and paten, (iv) fonts, pulpits and altars, (v) the blessing of the Font on Easter Eve, and (vi) a monarch, during the coronation.

Aspects of Confirmation are (i) completing, or firming up, or sealing, the baptism, as a farmer would seal a graft of a branch onto a trunk. The sap stays in and the germs stay out. Baptism is the graft, Confirmation is the seal. (ii) the confirmand has the opportunity to profess his faith in Christ and on his own, make the promises that were made for him in Baptism. (iii) Baptism is the bestowal of the Holy Spirit in general; Confirmation is the bestowal of the Holy Spirit for this particular person, for the unique vocation he is going to have — an equipping of the Holy Spirit for the unique ministry that is opening up for him. Fr. Schmemann used to say that the Seven-fold gift of the Holy Spirit in Confirmation is so that we can live our Christian life "with class." (iv) ordination to the Laity (v) making explicit the apostolic nature of the confirmand's ministry, since the hands of the bishop are the hands of an apostle.

p. 299, The first rubric indicates that now it is time for First Communion. The second rubric was found to be necessary in the 1789 book, since there were by 1789 only three or four bishops in the United States, which was not a sufficient number to minister to all who were ready to be confirmed. So if more than a tiny number were to be able to receive Communion, they could do so if they were "ready and desirous." Before 1789, George Washington, for example, was never confirmed, because he could not make the trip to London. But he was "ready and desirous," and so did receive Holy Communion. We have used this rubric in the *ekonomia* of the Church to allow people to receive Holy Communion who are ready and desirous to be confirmed.

Question: what hymns in the 1940 Hymnal would be suitable at a service (of either Holy Communion or Evening Prayer) at which Confirmation is administered?

In some places the **Solemnization of Matrimony** takes place at the very beginning of the Liturgy, and is followed by the Nuptial Eucharist. Other places follow the Vatican II reform, and put the wedding service after the Gospel in the Mass, and then go from the wedding service to the offertory of the Mass. (There is no Nicene Creed at weddings)

p. 300, The rubric at the top says that weddings should be held in the church, except for grave cause.

p. 300, The Exhortation, that begins "Dearly beloved," omits some very good material from the 1662 BCP. If you have a copy of the 1662 BCP, compare this Exhortation with the older one.

p. 301, Compare these vows with the 1662. Some very good things are omitted in the 1928 Book. The '28 vows omit, for the woman, the promise to obey her husband, and for the man, "with my body I thee worship." Many young couples today ask for the 1662 wedding service.

p. 302, The blessing of the ring: in the older services, there is only one ring, given by the Bridegroom to the Bride. This is because she *is* the marriage. She is the bearer of the marriage.

The husband is the transcendent element from beyond, who is the provider, protector and priest of the wife and marriage.

p. 303, The rubric at the bottom of the page says that with the joining of the hands, the priest may wrap the joined hands with the ends of his stole, and then raise their hands up, with the words "Those whom God hath joined together…"

p. 304, The Banns, and the form used for publishing them: they are printed out in the bulletin, and read out from the pulpit, for 3 Sundays in a row, prior to the wedding, to give relatives, parishioners, friends and neighbors, a chance to voice an objection (a "bann.")

p. 267, Here are the Propers for a Nuptial Mass. The Collect was written for the '28 Book.

p. 305, **The Churching of Women** is a beautiful service that has as its origin the presentation in the Temple of new born children and their mothers. The Service can be used after the Creed at Mass, or in the hospital, or in the mother's home.

Question—what do our Canons require of a couple coming to the priest to set up a wedding?

p. 308, **The Visitation of the Sick** was partly re-worked for the 1928 BCP. The earlier emphasis was on sickness as a chastisement to be borne. The new emphasis is on healing and recovery, or acceptance of fatal illness in a spirit of victory. Any part, or even all, of this Order may be used, keeping in mind that most sick people have a short attention span, and, in the hospital, there may be only three or four minutes with a sick person before nurses have to intervene with treatments.

p. 313, There is a rubric here which is the second time the BCP mentions sacramental confession to a priest. What follows on pp. 313 and 314 is almost like an absolution.

p. 317, This is the second of three Litanies in the PB.

p. 320, **Holy Unction** was added in 1928. If administered in conjunction with Holy Communion, the Eucharist is administered first, then Holy Unction. The oil used is the Oil of the Sick.

The rubric at the bottom of p. 320 is so that people know to include the church in their wills.

p. 321, This order for **The Communion of the Sick** presupposes an actual celebration of Holy Communion at a person's bed side, omitting what the rubrics say can be omitted. This abbreviated Eucharist would take about fifteen minutes, and is not easily done in a hospital room, but is sometimes advisable in a person's home, where that person is housebound and can profit from hearing more of the service they know well and likely miss very much. Of course in this format, both bread and wine are consecrated. Some clergy have a sick communion kit containing everything needed for a private celebration.

When administering Holy Communion from the Reserved Sacrament, the priest can adapt what is in the Prayer Book, so as to take only about five minutes, or use, or adapt, what is in *A Manual for Priests*. Holy Communion from the Reserved Sacrament (administering only the Body of Christ) is the normal way for the sick to receive this Sacrament. The Precious Blood is not reserved or carried about because it can spoil so easily, or be spilled.

Here is one possible format for administering Holy Communion from the Reserved Sacrament:

    (i)    Greet the person with the words at the top of p. 308, "Peace be to this house, (or place) and to all that dwell in it."

(ii) Say the Collect for the Day, or one of the Collects on pp. 309–317.
(iii) Use the Confession and Absolution on p. 323
(iv) Say the first two Comfortable Words, p. 76,
(v) Then the Our Father (together), and "Behold the Lamb of God…" and (once), "Lord I am not worthy…" and then the words of administration of the Host.
(vi) Finally, the first four verses of the Benedict, anima mea, (Psalm 103) with the Gloria Patri, or else the post communion thanksgiving (p. 83) followed by the Blessing (p. 84)

p. 323, There is an interesting rubric here about "Spiritual Communion," especially significant in times of plague, pestilence, war and separation from one's home or church.

Questions: Do you think it would be important to give an annual, or twice-yearly, sermon and/or a teaching on Holy Unction and healing (and facing terminal illness) that includes the material on pp. 308–323? How many reasons can you give for doing this? On what Sundays could this be tied in with the Gospel for the day?

p. 324, **The Order for the Burial of the Dead** is a revision of the old Mattins for the Dead.

With regard to the first rubric on p. 324, it is important to have the body brought in for the Liturgy, if at all possible. Undertakers are happy to comply with this, and do a cremation or burial after the Liturgy, but all this needs to be set up with the family and the undertaker in advance.

The second rubric on p. 324 refers to the psalms used. In accordance with Western Catholic usage, the Missals and other service books replace the Gloria Patri at the end of psalms with "Rest eternal grant unto them O Lord, and may light perpetual shine upon them."

p. 331, This rubric allows the Apostles' Creed and Our Father to go after the Lesson.

pp. 332–333, What is here, for the burial of the body, can be used as is for the interment of ashes. The rest of the Liturgy is self explanatory.

The Burial Office is sometimes done as a stand-alone office. But if there is a Requiem Mass, it follows the Burial Office, perhaps with a hymn in between. After the Requiem Mass comes the Absolution of the Body, from the *Priest's Manual*. The rubrics there are quite clear. After the Absolution of the Body, the casket is led in procession to the hearse, and taken to the cemetery for burial, or removed for cremation and a later interment.

pp. 338–342, The rubrics for **The Burial of a Child** are clear.

# THE PSALTER

R. M. Benson, the 19th century founder of the Cowley Fathers, near Oxford, England, called the Psalter "the war songs of the Prince of Peace."

p. 345, Our Psalter is not from the King James Bible, but from the Coverdale Bible of 1535, translated by Myles Coverdale. This Psalter passed into the 1549 BCP, and was kept in 1662, after the King James Bible was published, since the Coverdale Psalter is metrically better for chanting. In 1928 a few minor archaisms were eased out of it. The Coverdale is arguably the greatest English translation of the Psalter ever made. 16th English was, as Robert McNeill, in his TV series, *The Story of English* (p. 88) has noted, "zestful and vigourous, highly coloured, playful, self-confident and bursting with innovation."

For review, the 4 ways to choose psalms for the Daily Office are:

(i) The Lectionary–what is appointed for a given day, using, for saints' days and holy days that part of the Lectionary which pertains to them.
(ii) The "Daily Grind," psalms for Day 1, Day 2, etc, such that we read all 150 Psalms in a month.
(iii) "Selections of Psalms" from p. ix, psalms arranged thematically.
(iv) Officiant's choice.

On saints' days and holy days for which the BCP has propers, do please choose the psalm(s) from the Lectionary, under the heading, "Psalms and Lessons for the Fixed Holy Days."

Otherwise, if Ascension Day falls on the 4th of the month, and you are using the "Daily Grind," you will be reading Psalm 22 on the Feast of our Lord's Ascension. You do not want to use Psalm 109, EP for Day 22, if Thanksgiving falls on that day! One of the great features of the 1943 Lectionary we use in the 1928 BCP is the Lectionary's keeping with the theme of the day. So, for example, on Epiphany Day, January 6, the Psalms and readings are all about Christ revealed to the Gentiles. And on the Rogation Days, after Easter V, the Psalms and lessons are beautifully coordinated with the Rogationtide themes. And so too with the Ember Days, and all the saints' and holy days.

Many parishes follow four monastic customs:

- There is a slight pause at the asterisk. The nature of Hebrew poetry is not to rhyme words. Rather, there is a principle of parallelism, of creating a verse with two sections, one of which either complements, or clarifies, or is the opposite, of the other.
- The Gloria Patri is said after every psalm, and after every section of Psalm 119, "the Rosary of the Psalter."
- All imprecatory verses are used, and we should teach our people why. The 1928 revisers created a space in the text, such that verses after the space can be omitted because they are too "harsh."

— Either we chant the psalms, or move toward doing so. The 1940 Hymnal has numerous Anglican and Plainsong chants for all the canticles, and numerous psalms used as canticles.
— Canticles are chanted in unison, and psalms, in monasteries and convents, are chanted antiphonally, from side to side, each side proclaiming to the other the wonderful works of God.

It is good to know something about the different kinds of psalms: praise and thanksgiving, songs of trust, confessions, laments, wisdom psalms, enthronement, or royal psalms, and the "Psalms of Ascents," (120-135)

A rule of thumb from some old preachers: one third of all the sermons they give are on the Old Testament, which of course includes the Psalter.

Questions: What are the imprecatory verses in the Psalms? Why do we use them? How do we interpret them? It is good to expose all this to view, and come to grips with it.

# THE ORDINAL

being the
Form of Making, Ordaining and Consecrating
Bishops, Priests and Deacons
*together with*
The Form of Consecration of a Church
An Office of Institution of Ministers

p. 529, The Ordinal begins a new section of the BCP, which Shepherd calls "The Pontifical" (Shepherd, p. xiii), or the services reserved for the Bishop. Prior to the BCP, the Pontifical was a separate book.

The other separate books that Cranmer put together to make up the BCP were the Breviary, for the Daily Offices, the Missal, for the Eucharist, the Manual, or Ritual, also sometimes called the Pastorale, for the Occasional Offices. In our 1928 BCP, these once separate books appear in this order: Breviary, Missal, Manual, Pontifical. To these original four separate books, the Catechism, Family Prayer and the Articles of Religion have been added. These additions were in the first American PB of 1789.

In our Ordinal, which first came out in 1550, no provision was made for the Minor Orders (doorkeeper, acolyte, exorcist, sub-deacon) Exercise of these minor orders was left to the Diocesan Bishop, and, in a sense, the Minor Orders were "laicized." It has long been a custom of Anglo-Catholics that a fully trained lay-reader (always a man) is a Sub-Deacon at a Solemn High Mass. In the colonial days in America, the "Clerk" (pronounced "clark") might be the Squire who founds the parish, pays for the construction of a church building, and goes on to lead Morning Prayer and the Litany most Sundays, and in the (frequent) lack of a Rector in residence, gives leadership in administrative and financial matters. Such a Clerk could be considered a de-facto Sub-deacon. In those days, "clerk" meant someone who could read. So you had "clerks," and "clerks in Holy Orders."

By 1804 the Form of Consecration of a Church or Chapel, and An Office of Institution of Ministers, were added to the 1789 American BCP.

Here are some common features of ordinations:

— The Eucharist is an integral part of every ordination for all three Orders.
— The Bishop alone ordains Deacons.
— The Bishop, with his College of Presbyters, ordains Priests, all of whom join in the laying on of hands.
— Three Bishops consecrate a new Bishop. That is the rule, although there are occasional exceptions to it.

During the Reformation, the essential action in ordaining—the laying on of hands—was retained. What is given to the ordinand is a Bible. Later, especially after the Oxford and Ritualist movements in 19th century England and America, some of the older ceremonies were brought back: the anointing of the Priest's hands with Chrism, the presentation of a chalice and paten, and the vesting (with eucharistic vestments) for the appropriate order. And for a Bishop, the bestowal of the crozier, mitre and ring.

p. 530, Ever since the 1662 BCP in England, Deacons are "made," Priests are "ordained," and Bishops are "consecrated."

**The Form and Manner of Making Deacons** begins with the Sermon, then goes on to the Presentation and Charge, and then the Litany for Ordinations, on p. 560, which was written for the 1928 American Book. This is the third Litany in the BCP, the other two being the Great Litany and the Litany for the Dying.

p. 531, After the Litany for Ordinations, usually chanted, the Communion Service begins with the Collect for Purity. At the end of the Epistle, the Ordination of the candidate(s) begins with the Exhortation, which sets forth the duties of the Deacon, liturgical, homiletical, catechetical and pastoral.

p. 534, The newly ordained Deacon reads the Gospel for the day, after which the Mass continues as usual. The new Deacon may, and usually does, assist in the administration of the Chalice, and pronounce the Dismissal before the Blessing.

After the Post-communion thanksgiving, the Bishop reads a Post-communion Collect. There are four times when the BCP provides a Post-communion Collect after the thanksgiving after Communion (p. 83) — when ordaining deacons, priests or bishops, and in consecrating a church. The Missal has a proper Post-communion for every Mass, along with an Introit, Gradual, Offertory Verse and Communion Verse, together known as the "Minor Propers." Luther kept all this; Cranmer did not. But our Post communion thanksgiving on

p. 83, used at every Mass, is a phenomenal and incomparable masterpiece, theologically, liturgically and aesthetically.

Whenever possible, ordinations take place on one of the Ember Days. Here is some background on these days, on what they mean, and how they came into use.

We see in Acts 1: 12-28 how the Apostles gather and pray as they choose Matthias to replace Judas. In Acts 13: 1-4, the Church in Antioch gathers, and "while they were worshiping the Lord and fasting, the Holy Spirit said, 'Set apart for me Barnabas and Saul for the work for which I have called them.' Then after fasting and praying they laid their hands on them and sent them off. So, being sent out by the Holy Spirit, they went down to Seleucia; and from there they sailed to Cypress."

By the time of Pope Gregory the Great in the late 6th century there were fixed times of prayer and fasting for those preparing for Holy Orders, and for those who were being ordained at these fixed times, which occurred four times a year, as a Wednesday, Friday and Saturday (i) after the Feast of St. Lucy (December 13), (ii) after the First Sunday in Lent (iii) after the Feast of Pentecost and (iv) after Holy Cross Day (September 14). The Ember Days have a penitential aspect to them, and so the color is violet.

The Ember Days have, for the Daily Office, their own Psalms and Lessons in our Lectionary, on pp. x, xi, xviii, xix, xxiv, xxv, xl and xli. Also for the Daily Office are the prayers on the bottom of p. 38 and the top of p. 39. It is also possible, after the Collects in Morning or Evening Prayer, to use the Litany for Ordinations on p. 560.

The Propers for the Eucharist begin on p. 260, appointed for all 12 Ember Days. The Missal appoints different propers for each of them. Some clergy prefer to use the Prayer Book ones, so that people know that they are there, and can make use of them at home, and some clergy use the Missal propers, for greater variety.

The Collect has a modern feel to it, with some mid-19th century authorship. It was first used publicly in the 1928 Book, and includes the phrase "ministry of reconciliation" from 2 Cor. 5: 18. The Epistle, from Acts 13, has a missionary theme. The Gospel, from Luke 4, with Jesus in the synagogue, is, one might say, our Lord's inaugural address, with the agenda for the Anointed One, and for those whom He sends out.

In the various inter-woven themes of the Ember Days, we include prayer for seminarians and the seminaries they attend, for those who teach and those who learn, for bishops who will be ordaining men, for those being ordained on the Ember Days (we try if possible, to ordain on the days when the Church is praying and fasting), for the increase of the ministry (p. 39), for missions (p. 38) and for all lay ministry.

Really teaching about and observing the Ember Days is a stepping stone to the recovery of fullness of life in Christ, driving home the centrality of apostolic ministry, and the eternal Gospel we proclaim.

There is speculation about the name, "Ember Day," or "Embertide." "Ember" is one of the many nick-names we have in the Family of God, such as "Christmas," and "Lent," and the word "Mass." It is entirely possible that "Ember" is an Anglicization of the French, *Quatre Temps*, or "Four Times." When our Anglo-Saxon ancestors heard *Quatre Temps* from the Norman invaders, they processed only the "emps" and made it sound more Germanic, as in "Ember." The Anglo-Saxons processed most French words and names in this way. "Beauchamps" becomes "beechum," etc.

Let us say that during one year, the Vigil of St. Thomas the Apostle, December 21, is an Ember Wednesday in Advent. Saying all the Collects would result in (i) the Collect for St. Thomas, (ii) the Collect for Ember Day, (iii) the Collect for Advent 3, and (iv) the Collect for Advent Season. It could well be pastorally and liturgically appropriate to omit (iii) and (iv).

Finally, seminarians and postulants for Holy Orders are, at each of the four Ember Seasons, to report to the Bishop in writing on their academic progress and manner of life and other matters of concern or interest.

Now we return to the Ordering of Deacons. The rubric on p. 535 states that a Deacon serves in this Order for a year, which may be shortened by the Bishop.

p. 536, Here, in **The Form and Manner of Ordering Priests**, and on p. 530 & 552, the bishop is addressed as "Father." In England it is still normal to call the bishop "Father." Until the late 19th century priests were called "Mister," or "Doctor," if they had that degree. This could also be the case in France, where the title *Monsieur* was sometimes used, and from which, of course, is derived "monsignor." It is thought that the use of the title "Father" for priests came from Ireland, where it was taken over in England by the clergy involved in the Tractarian and Ritualist Movements, following on the heels of the Oxford Movement. Today it is providential that the title has become widespread for priests, because of the feminist attack on patriarchy, fatherhood and the family.

p. 539, This Exhortation and Examination for the ordinands is a masterpiece, and a virtual commentary on the Gospel preceding it, on p. 538, taken from John 10: 1ff. "The glory of authorship goes to Cranmer," and Shepherd calls it "an expression of his highest ideals for the personal and pastoral side of the priest's office, such as has never been equaled." (*Commentary*, p. 540)

p. 543, Here we have the *Veni, Creator Spiritus*, one of the most famous early medieval hymns, the only metrical hymn in the PB (#217 in the 1940 Hymnal). The 1940 Hymnal has most of the others, eg, *Victimae Paschali*, # 97, *The Golden Sequence,* # 109, *Dies Irae,* # 468, and others. Using the *Veni, Creator Spiritus* before the Ordination is *epicletic*, along with the *Epiclesis* in the Eucharistic Canon, and the short prayer in the Missal before the Gospel ("Cleanse my heart and my lips, O thou Almighty God, as thou didst purge the lips of the Prophet Isaiah with a live coal, that I may rightly and worthily proclaim thy holy Gospel.") In some places, the *Veni, Creator* is used at Confirmations.

p. 546–"Receive the Holy Ghost for the Office and Work…" Office relates to who the priest is, to his being, his ontology, as an icon of Christ. "Work," or "function," relates to what the priest does. "Being" and "doing" are consubstantial. In both "being" and "doing," in Christ, the priest reveals to every man his priesthood. The priest models the essence of redeemed patriarchy, which is both gracious and kenotic.

p. 547, Another instance of a special Post-communion Prayer after the generally used one on p. 83.

p. 552, In **The Form of Ordaining or Consecrating a Bishop**, The Testimonials show the corporate nature of the Church, viz., (i) evidence of canonical election by the Synod where the newly consecrated bishop is to serve, (ii) evidence of ordination to the Diaconate and Priesthood, (iii) consents of the majority of the Standing Committees of all the dioceses of the Church and (iv) consents of a majority of the Bishops of the Church.

p. 554, In the Examination there is a strong emphasis on the Bishop′s guardianship of the Faith.

p. 560, **The Litany and Suffrages for Ordinations** is the third Litany in the BCP, added in 1928 as an alternative to the Great Litany. Like most of what was composed for the '28 Book, it has a slightly modern feel to it.

p. 563, **The Form of Consecration of a Church or Chapel** was composed by Convocation in the Church of England in 1712, and adopted in the American BCP after the 1789 Book came out. It shows a Reformation characteristic of preferring to bless people rather than things. The use of this Service would spread in the colonies, as new churches were constantly being built.

p. 569, **An Office of Institution of Ministers** was adopted in the United States. in 1804. In the letter to the new incumbent, the Bishop gives expression to the *perichoretic* relationship between himself, the Rector and the Congregation.

Question: What does *perichoretic* mean? Hint: it is more or less the Greek equivalent of the Latin word *consubstantial.*

p. 572, It is interesting to note that the first prayer is addressed to God the Father, the second, to God the Son, and the third, to God the Holy Ghost. The third prayer is quite useful at Vestry and Annual Parish Meetings.

p. 573, In the first rubric is the restoration of the word *Altar*. Here we have the first instance of this word appearing in a BCP since 1552. The use of this word, on this page, is the only instance of its use in the 1928 BCP. The Prayer on this page is most suitable in the Priest's life whenever he wishes to re-consecrate his ministry to our Lord, the great High-Priest.

p. 574, In the first rubric is the first instance of the use of the word *Eucharist* in any version of the BCP. In fact, one has to go back much further to find any use of this word in a Prayer Book or Missal. The word is now liturgically restored, and will be used with greater frequency in the coming generations, opening wider the door to a *patristic* understanding of the Holy Mysteries.

# A CATECHISM

p. 577, This Catechism is one of the shorter ones produced during the Reformation. Based on the Apostles'Creed, the Ten Commandments and the Lord's Prayer...what to believe, how to live, and how to pray. The Rector is the ultimately responsible person for making sure everyone in his congregation is properly catechized. A youthful mind, applied with diligence, can memorize this Catechism. The memory work is made easier by the classical language. Most clergy will present for confirmation anyone who at least knows the Apostles'Creed, the Decalogue and the Our Father by heart, with some key phrases of the Catechism thrown in, and some other background material.

It is likely that Cranmer had at least a hand in the first part of our Catechism, p. 577 to the top of p. 581. The last part, about the Sacraments, was added by the Hampton Court Conference of 1604. Our Catechism was, in a sense, enlarged in 1928, with the introduction of the Offices of Instruction (pp. 283-295) thus making the Catechism into a liturgical service in two parts. Pages 290-291 and 294-295 are entirely new, with material on the Church and the Ministry.

These Offices, or the old Catechism, can be used occasionally in place of a sermon, perhaps during Trinitytide. If the Rector has to be absent, a lay-reader or deacon can lead in one of the Offices of Instruction or the Catechism. We should encourage parents to do the same with their children at home, and become familiar with both the Offices of Instruction and the Catechism.

The author has never been bothered by the answer for the question, "How many Sacraments hath Christ ordained in his Church? Two only, as generally necessary for salvation; that is to say, Baptism and the Supper of the Lord." First of all this is true, with the phrase, "as generally necessary to salvation." Secondly, we may teach, with the Fathers, that Confession and Confirmation are part of Baptism, and that Matrimony, Unction and Orders are part of the Eucharist... the Marriage Supper of the Lamb...the sacrament of healing *par excellence*...Orders being instituted to reveal the Church in the Eucharist.

Thirdly, one can teach that there is one Sacrament, *the Church*, the Sacrament of the Holy Spirit, the Bride from whom all the mysteries flow. Or, that there are two Sacraments, Baptism and the Eucharist, the other five inhering in them. Or one can teach that there are seven Sacraments, the medieval synthesis, seven being the number of completion. Or that there are thousands of sacraments, such as preaching, coronation of a monarch, and what Rome calls "sacramentals," such as Holy Water, making the sign of the Cross, and so on. The Eastern Fathers would say that with the Atonement, all creation is now a means of communion with the Father, through the Son, in the Holy Spirit. So once something is received with thanksgiving (blessing something by giving thanks for it)...once something is offered eucharistically to the Father, through the Son, in the Holy Spirit, it becomes a means of communion with the triune God, and with one another in Him. The Eucharist is the ultimate manifestation of this, because with bread and wine, we are, in union with Jesus' perfect offering, returning ourselves, and all creation to the Father, in the Holy Spirit. A cigar, in Christ, now becomes a sacrament of contentment and prosperity.

One of the fruits of the Oxford Movement was a late 19th–early 20th century series called *The Oxford Library of Practical Theology*, edited by the Rev. W. C. E. Newbolt and the Rev. Darwell Stone. One of the many volumes in this series is *The Church Catechism, The Christian's Manual*, by W. C. E. Newbolt. Somewhere in this book he indicates an *ascetical progression* in the old Catechism. We begin with "What is your Name?" We begin therefore with *the person*, *the person* who is answering. We begin with *me*. We end with "be in charity with all men." We have gone through an ascetical progression from the person, to the corporate whole, all wrapped up in the love of God. From this we can distill the whole of Christian ascesis, the movement, inspired and sustained by the love of God, from the purgative way, through the illuminative way, to the unitive way.

p. 582-583, These rubrics are of utmost importance to all rectors and vicars — all who have "the cure of souls." These rubrics have, of course, been sorely neglected for generations. We have statistics of how many, or how few, can name all four Evangelists, or all the books of the Bible, or the Seven Sacraments, and the list goes on. Over the years, I have taken, as the beginning of a remedy, two things, each one sentence long, that every Christian should know: the Gospel in one sentence, and the aim of the Christian life. Knowing just these two things provides pegs on which to hang everything else.

*Questions:* In one sentence, or phrase, what is the aim of the Christian life? What is the Gospel, in one sentence, or phrase? There are numerous ways to answer these questions.

# FAMILY PRAYER

p. 587, Forms of Prayer to be used in Families, wss introduced in 1789, and the "Additional Prayers" was added in 1928. Quoting from Shepherd, "These prayers (pp. 587–591) were composed by Edmund Gibson, while he was rector of Lambeth...Gibson became Bishop of London in 1723, and in this capacity he had ecclesiastical jurisdiction over the Church in the American colonies until his death in 1748...A friend of the Wesleys...he was a diligent and faithful pastor, and had particular concern for the conversion of Negroes on the colonial plantations...his little book of family devotions was especially popular...In the colonies, where the Society for the Propagation of the Gospel (SPG) promoted its distribution, it met a very real need, since many families of church people were cut off from regular participation in Common Prayer..."

"Both in style and in content these prayers are the finest contribution of eighteenth-century piety to the Prayer Book. Phrases from the Bible and the Prayer Book are subtly interwoven into the flow of their serene, but no less searching eloquence. They are a free paraphrase and commentary upon the constant elements of the Daily Offices—penitence, supplication, and thanksgiving—combining with consummate art deep personal feeling and apt expression of corporate love and need."

p. 591, The Thanksgiving–It is good for our people to memorize this, to add to their repertoire of thanksgivings (p. 33, p. 48 [the conclusion of the Bidding Prayer] and pp. 50–53, and of course p. 83), so that we grow in eucharistic living…"in everything giv(ing) thanks," thanks for the mercy promised to our forefathers, now performed in our lives. The General Thanksgiving on p. 33 and the Post Communion Thanksgiving on p. 83 are each absolute masterpieces, biblically, theologically, liturgically and aesthetically. The Thanksgiving on p. 591 adds a personal touch, or application, to them.

p. 592–593, A Shorter Form. Again, quoting from Shepherd, "The speed and haste of modern life, pressing with particular force on the family circle, doubtless induced the 1928 revisers to provide this minimum form of family devotions, drawn from the Daily Offices…"

pp. 594–600, all 25 of these Additional Prayers were added in the 1928 revision. "Though some of them are distinctly personal or serviceable only in intimate groups such as the family, many of them are useful supplements to the materials afforded in the occasional Prayers and Thanksgivings, beginning on p. 35. The first six concern the spirit and occasions of worship, the next five, various spiritual graces. Then follow eight intercessions for persons near and dear to us and four for our common life in society. Two table blessings conclude this section." (Shepherd, p. 594)

p. 596, For the Absent, a prayer that was used constantly for public worship in WWII, along with the prayer following it. It is possible, after the words "bless those whom we love, now absent from us," to insert the names of those for whom we are praying.

p. 597, For a Birthday. Many parishes invite people celebrating birthdays and other anniversaries to stand, or come forward, perhaps after the Creed, or after Communion, and have this prayer said over them. It has to be one of the best prayers ever composed for a birthday. It can, of course, be used at a birthday party.

# THE ARTICLES OF RELIGION

pp. 601–611, When the 1789 BCP was composed, no Articles were put in it. They were added in 1801. Quoting from Shepherd, "The Church was not of one mind regarding their value or necessity." (p. 601)

The promulgation of articles or confessional statements (the great confessions being the Augsburg for Lutherans in 1530, and the Westminster in 1552, for Calvinists) was a feature of the Reformation. Today we have, in our ranks, these permitted views:

(i) the Articles are of little value today, because we are no longer facing Reformation issues, but rather the crises of the 3rd and 4th centuries, centering on the Incarnation. This position is found mostly among ardent Anglo-Catholics.

(v) the Articles are important as historical documents, as a way of clarifying issues which are part of our heritage. With heresy swirling about us today, the Articles are like a handbrake on a car. John Henry Newman (a father of the 19th century Oxford Movement) taught us how to interpret Articles like number 25 in a Catholic way.

(iii) the Articles are vital to our life as Anglicans, and should be augmented, so that we can become more confessional...a position taken mostly by evangelicals.

This author writes from the vantage point of (ii), above, this probably being the majority view among traditional, orthodox Anglicans around the world. Although we have occasional confessional sympathies, the ecclesiology of Anglicanism is essentially conciliar. When we start looking at Canon Law below, we will begin to address the various ecclesiologies in the Church:

(i) Magisterial (the Roman system, with a teaching *magisterium* in Rome, centered in the Pope)
(vi) Confessional (the system of the magisterial reformers, defining and systematizing doctrine)
(vii) Congregational, with the local congregation deciding all matters of faith and practice
(viii) Conciliar (the system of the undivided Church of the first millennium, and today, of all the Orthodox, and ourselves, who are as likely to be *symphonic* theologians as *systematic*.

Our Articles are, to quote Shepherd, "directed against the errors of the medieval Latin Church on the one side, and the aberrations of the Anabaptist sects on the other. Likewise they avoid taking a definite side with the peculiar doctrines either of Lutheranism or of Calvinism, although in general, they are nearer the former than the latter...They are Protestant to the extent that they do not claim any doctrines as necessary to salvation except those that can be proved and established by the Holy Scriptures, but they are also Catholic in the sense that they do not reject the developed traditions of the undivided Church of the early centuries that are in accord with the mind of Scripture. In any case they reject the claims of any church or sect to be infallible and unerring in matters of Faith or in its living and manner of Ceremonies (cf. Article 19).

"Inasmuch as the Articles are but one part of the Prayer Book, it is important to remember that the doctrine of the Anglican communion is enshrined in the Prayer Book as a whole. The Articles should be interpreted in the light of the teaching of the entire Prayer Book. They are not a norm by which the rest of the Prayer Book must of necessity be judged and explained." (p. 601)

# NOTES ON EUCHARISTIC THEOLOGY AND CUSTOMS

Dom Gregory Dix's *The Shape of the Liturgy* was much acclaimed when it came out in 1945. Dix, an Anglican Benedictine, was eager to get beyond or behind the 1662 Rite, to a pure source, which he saw as something akin to the Hippolytan Rite of St. Hippolytus of Rome (235 AD). An uninterrupted 4-fold shape in the Liturgy was critical to Dix, going without interruption from Offertory, to Consecration, to Fraction to Communion: "Taking, Blessing, Breaking and Giving." His instinct for this was part of the great 20th century reform of the Western Rite, finally enunciated by Vatican II, in the *Novus Ordo,* and in the Episcopal Church, in Rites I and II.

Dix suspected that Cranmer was a Zwinglian and was influenced by receptionism. That explains some of his desire to get beyond and behind the reformers. But I do not believe Cranmer was a Zwinglian, one reason for this being Cranmer's thoroughly catholic, and patristic, Prayer of Humble Access, which has all the sacramental realism of John 6. It helps to know that Dix was an Anglo-Papalist, unwilling to embrace anything that would hinder union with Rome.

Along with Dix in the mid-twentieth century, there was a strong movement among Roman Catholic theologians called the *ressourcement*, the return to sources, to the patristic consensus of the undivided Church. Many of these theologians concerned themselves with Liturgical Theology: Hans Urs von Balthasar (John Paul II's favorite theologian, and a commentator on Maximus the Confessor), Louis Bouyer, Yves Congar, Jean Danilou, Karl Rahner and Eduard Schillebeeckx. These were among the fathers of Vatican II, who moved the Roman Church more towards a "communion theology", and towards episcopal collegiality and conciliarity. But as Loudovikos shows in his book, *Church in the Making*, only preliminary steps have been taken by Vatican II toward an ecclesiology rooted in ontology. In other words, the Church has to be more than a mechanism for representing Christ.

Dix, and Vatican II, represent valid approaches to liturgical reform, and are in keeping with the Western concern for *systematic* and logical sequence. But Anglican Liturgy, growing largely from its ancient roots in the British and Sarum rites, is more Eastern, and *symphonic*, in its approach. Instead of going back to a "pure" source, our Liturgy is like a snowball rolling down a hill, picking up snow from every part of the hill as it rolls down. So we have elements of ancient rites, Eastern and Western, with a heavy dose of the patristic themes (our Canon has echoes of John 17), and then, the medieval emphasis, then the reformed, and the Caroline, and the modern, from the Wesleys through to the Oxford Movement and on into the luminaries of the 20th century such as C. S. Lewis, Eric Mascall, Martin Thornton, Alan Richardson and Michael Ramsey. The 4-fold shape is there, but more rounded and complex, such that, in the Offertory, we offer bread, wine, alms, intercessions, and our sins. Then we go on to the Sursum Corda and the Great Thanksgiving. Cranmer put the Fraction at the Words of Institution, and he put the Peace at the very end, as an introduction to the final Blessing.

Massey Shepherd, when his *Oxford American Prayer Book Commentary* was published in 1950, was moving toward the *ressourcement* school, but was still fully appreciative of the greatness of our 1928 Liturgy, which already has many *ressourcement* features and echoes of the Liturgy of St. John Chrysostom. When the Western Rite Antiochians recently published a Missal containing a "Liturgy of St. Tikhon," they used the *American Missal* (which incorporates the 1928 Rite) with virtually no changes except for the *Filioque* clause.

One of the greatest books on the Eucharist written in the 20th century, or perhaps ever, is Fr. Alexander Schmemann's *The Eucharist: Sacrament of the Kingdom*. Fr. Schmemann is part of the enormous 19th and 20th century revival of the patristic consensus among the Orthodox, breaking out of their own scholasticism for a full recovery of what it means to be the Church, and to explore the mystery of the Eucharist as constitutive of the Church. Nicholas Afanasiev, with his eucharistic ecclesiology, was part of this revival, as is John Zizioulas, with his ground-breaking *Being as Communion*, and Zizioulas' pupil in Thessaloniki, Nikolaus Loudovikos with his *Church in the Making*, eliciting for us the full benefits of the theology of St. Maximus the Confessor, a theology and philosophy that can help us in the West to overcome the dialectics which have ham-strung us since Hegel. Word and Sacrament, for example, do not have to be in dialectical tension, or seen as antinomies. They are, as Loudovikos and Maximus would say, consubstantial and perichoretic and co-inherent. They are in dialogical reciprocity with each other. So are other tensions and "polar opposites" so often posited: universal–local, or Geist–Amt, or freedom–necessity, or clergy–laity, or personal–corporate, or sacred–secular, systematic–symphonic, and so on.

## Questions that arise, and matters of interest

—What is the difference between the American and Anglican Missals? The differences in these two Missals are slight. I like one for some of its unique features, and the other, for its. For example, the pointing for the chanting of the *Exsultet* on Easter Eve is, I think, ever so slightly better in the *Anglican Missal*. The lay-out of text on the pages is slightly better in the American.

A parish church is better off with the *American Missal*, compiled in 1931 for parish use. So the Blessing of Ashes on Ash Wednesday, or of Palms, on Palm Sunday, is shorter and more suited to a parish community. The priest who revised the *American Missal* in 1950, Fr. Earle Hewitt Maddux, SSJE, also compiled *A Manual for Priests*, and so blessings in one are the same as in the other.

There is a new 2010 edition of the *American Missal*, compiled by the Lancelot Andrewes Press of the Western Rite of the Antiochian Orthodox Church, beautifully bound and reasonably priced. It is the most comprehensive *American Missal* ever compiled, because it not only has the eucharistic rite of the *American Missal*, it adds the Gregorian Canon in English and Latin, the 1549 Canon, and the Rite of St. Tikhon, which is the Anglican rite, omitting the filioque clause in the Creed, and adding a few things that the Orthodox like. Interestingly, it leaves things like the Epiclesis in our '28 Canon entirely unchanged. There are some additional propers and proper prefaces. The Lancelot Andrewes Press has also made available a revision of the 1928 BCP which I think moves toward what we would want in a '28 revision.

The *Anglican Missal* is perhaps drafted with monastic communities in mind. So there are fewer time constraints with blessing things. The Blessing of Ashes or the Blessing of Palms, or of the New Fire and Paschal Candle for example are very fulsome. When all I have is the *Anglican Missal*, I omit at least half what is proposed. The *Anglican Missal* is available in pew size, with very useful annotations and commentary, and is called *The People's Anglican Missal*, available from the Anglican Parishes Association in Athens, Georgia, for somewhat less than 30 dollars.

Note that in all these Missals and Prayer Books, the right hand margins are justified, symbolizing permanence and confidence. Modern liturgical texts often have unjustified right hand margins, which may suggest that the text is ragged, fluctuating and provisional.

—The '28 BCP mentions sacramental confession in three places. Do you know where to find them?

- (i) In the 2nd Exhortation, on the top of p. 88. "therefore, if there be any of you., who by this means cannot quiet his own conscience herein, but requireth further comfort or counsel, let him come to me, or to some other Minister of God's Word, and open his grief; that he may receive such godly counsel and advice, as may tend to the quieting of his conscience, and the removal of all scruple and doubtfulness."
- (ii) In the rubric on p. 313 in the Visitation of the Sick: "Then shall the sick person be moved to make a special confession of his sins, if he feel his conscience troubled by any matter; after which confession, on evidence of his repentance, the

> Minister shall assure him of God's mercy and forgiveness."
>
> (iii) In the Ordering of Priests, on p. 546, paraphrasing from John 20: 23, "Whose sins thou dost forgive, they are forgiven; and whose sins thou dost retain, they are retained."

Note, in the Visitation of the Sick, on p. 313 at the bottom, and all of p. 314, that these prayers are virtually an absolution. It is possible to use these prayers in hearing a confession, and to add an actual absolution from p. 24.

The Rite we most frequently use for hearing confessions comes from *A Manual for Priests*, taken from the 1662 BCP of the C of E, and from Western usage. The C of E prayer of absolution is "Our Lord Jesus Christ, who has left power to his Church to absolve all sinners who truly repent and believe in him, of his great mercy, and by his authority committed unto me, I + absolve thee from all thy sins, in the Name of the Father, and of the Son, and of the Holy Ghost. Amen."

—Must the Cross on the Altar be a crucifix? Most of our parishes have a Crucifix over the Altar. But the Sarum use in pre-Reformation England was to have an ornate, jeweled Resurrection Cross on the Altar. The Crucifix, the Rood, was on top of the Rood Screen (a carved wood screen with fairly wide openings, easily seen through, that separates the Chancel from the Nave, in the same place where an Iconostasis would be in an Orthodox church). Very often the Crucifix is flanked by carved statues of Our Lady and the Beloved Disciple. In order to receive Holy Communion, the people go through the wide opening in the middle of the Rood Screen, and so go through, and under the Blood, to the Holy of holies, to where the risen Lord is.

The Crucifix would also hang somewhere behind the Pulpit, because "we preach Christ crucified." (I Cor. 1: 23)

A Sarum Altar in a town church for 300-400 people would be very large, perhaps 10 feet wide, with the jeweled Resurrection Cross and two large candles on it. Behind, and on both sides flanking the Altar, would be a Riddle Curtain, some 10 feet high, with candles on top, sometimes held by carved angels. A Reredos, carved in wood or stone, full of saints´ figures, would be behind the Altar, above the Riddle Curtain, and above that, the East Window, in stained glass. The Tabernacle would be off to one side, with a Sanctuary Lamp hanging in front of it. On steps in front of the Altar, processional torches or other tall candles would be placed. A tower for such a church would have a "change" of great bells, one of which is rung for the Sanctus and the Consecration, and all of which are rung before and after all liturgies, in elaborate systems of "ringing the changes" as a way of communicating to all within earshot, whether the Liturgy is a Mass, a baptism, a wedding or a funeral, the Angelus or a warning for the approach of flood waters or enemies.

To see all this on line, look up Westminster Abbey or Southwark Cathedral, both in London. St. Paul´s Cathedral in London is not Sarum, but Baroque.

For another treat, to further explore the wonders and true powers of the ancient bells in English church towers, have a look at the BBC´s "The Nine Taylors," with Lord Peter Wimsey, based on one of Dorothy Sayer´s novels of that name. These dvds are available from Acorn Media, on Amazon of course. "The Nine Taylors" takes place just after WWI in East Anglia, where Dorothy Sayers shows the C of E, and one of her noble vicars, at their absolute best.

# NOTES ON THE 1940 HYMNAL

This Hymnal has been widely appreciated for being thoroughly catholic, in that it uses hymnody from every era of the Church's history, drawing from a wide variety of cultures: American, English, Irish, Scandinavian, Dutch, German, French, Italian, Russian and Greek. 48 new American and Canadian tunes were added in 1940.

The best version to have on hand is "*The Hymnal 1940 With Supplements I and II*," available for about 30 dollars from Amazon. *Supplement I* was added in 1960, and *Supplement II* in 1976. Altogether, this is the large red Hymnal we have in many of our pews.

We can see on p. vii, from the Contents, that there is a clear, logical arrangement of hymns, and service music, with very useful indexes.

Some of the indexes used on a weekly basis are on p. 799–803, Subject and Topical Indexes for selecting hymns by those methods, and on p. 804–806, for selecting hymns according to the themes presented on Sundays or Holy Days. In this latter section, "An effort has been made to use hymns that would lend some degree of liturgical unity to the services of the Church."

In selecting hymns, some clergy, organists and choir directors have a list of people's favorite hymns, which can be factored in when appropriate. After a generation or so a congregation develops a repertoire of material it favors, and sings well. This is all to the good, as long as there is an on-going effort to expand the repertoire of hymns and service music. One rule of thumb is that for every new hymn or new piece of service music, there should be three or four familiar pieces to keep the confidence of the singing congregation. As a congregation matures, we try to increase the amount of the Liturgy that is sung, starting out with the Ordinary of the Mass (Kyrie, Gloria, Sanctus and Agnus Dei) and adding, as we grow confident, a psalm after the Old Testament Lesson, the Epistle and Gospel, the Nicene Creed, an Offertory or Communion Anthem, and the Our Father. In the Daily Office we may start with hymns, and then go on to chanting the Preces, the Canticles, a Psalm or two, the Suffrages and the Collects.

At our Cathedral, in Lent and Advent, nine Sundays altogether, the Deacon of the Mass sings the Litany in Procession in place of the Introit Hymn, using the Ferial Tone. The Introit, or the Collect for Purity, follows on after the Litany. (Two tones for chants are Ferial, or simple, and Festal, or more complex)

Just how much a congregation can learn sometimes depends on whether or not there is a choir, or a schola, to give leadership. A small choral group (two or more) can learn to sing the Minor Propers at Mass (Introit, Gradual/Sequence, Offertory Verse and Communion Verse). The Minor Propers are not in the Hymnal, but are available upon request from various "Kyrials" and other compilations — the *St. Dunstan's Kyrial*, for example. A new book of service music and psalms has just come out of Dallas, Texas, from the Cathedral Church of the Holy Communion (Reformed Episcopal Church). If I am not mistaken, *The English Hymnal,* and *The New English Hymnal,* have the Minor Propers.

Some congregations have enjoyed occasional rehearsals *as an entire congregation.* At our Cathedral there is an occasional (six times a year or so) "Community Psalm Sing," on a Saturday morning, followed by lunch. A couple dozen of our people come, with their children, and often bring friends and neighbors. They are working through a Scottish Psalter and learning Anglican Chant and Plainsong as well. Our two most common ways to chant psalms, canticles and service music is with Anglican Chant and/or with Plainsong. *The Hymnal* has a good balance of these, starting on p. 601, with a rich stock of Plainsong hymns.

The Rector of a parish is always in charge of the music, although he may delegate some, or all, of this responsibility to an organist or music or choir director.

One fascinating book to get is *The Hymnal 1940 Companion,* annotating each hymn and section of service music with who wrote the words, and who composed the music, and under what circumstances, and why. Sometimes there will even be commentary on the choice of the tune's name.

Take, for example, Hymn 1, with the tune "Stuttgart." The *Companion* may say why that name was given to the tune. The best clue in passing is that the tune, written in Gotha, is German. Charles Wesley wrote the words, and all his hymns are theological and devotional masterpieces.

This is a great hymn with which to begin *The Hymnal*...a great hymn for the First Sunday in Advent.

To see what other hymns Charles Wesley wrote (17 more of which are in *The Hymnal*), go to p. 810 of the "Index of Authors, Translators, Sources."

Our Hymnal has two kinds of music for psalms and canticles:

Plainsong, sometimes associated with Pope St. Gregory the Great (6th cent), is also used in hymns like # 2, 6, 8, etc. Chants for the Nicene Creed, the Sursum Corda ("Lift up your hearts") and the Our Father are often Plainsong. The earliest known hymns are in the Hymnal as Office and Sequence hymns, listed on p. 830 at the bottom. Some of the Office Hymns were written by St. Ambrose in the 4th century, viz,, 158, 1st tune, *Splendor Paternae*. Examples of Sequence Hymns are 97, *Victimae Paschali*, 217, *Veni Creator*, and 468, *Dies Irae*. Most of the hymnody of the early Church consisted in the use of the Psalms. Proliferation of hymns not taken word for word from the Bible began gradually in the Reformation and accelerated from the 17th century onwards.

Anglican Chant grew out of the late 17th century English cathedral choir tradition as an adaptation of Plainsong, and flourished in the 19th and 20th centuries, spreading throughout the Anglican Communion and beyond. You may want to go to Amazon and type in something like "Psalms–Anglican Chant–Westminster Abbey," or "Psalms–Anglican Chant–King's College Cambridge," and order a CD or two, and prepare for a feast.

As we use the Hymnal in conjunction with our Cathedral congregation we continually learn wonderful new things. For example, Hymn 64 is often used on Palm Sunday. The 2nd and 3rd tunes for this are stout and dignified and good. But the 1st tune, *The King's Majesty*, composed in 1940 for the (then) new Hymnal, is an absolute masterpiece, revealing onomatapoetically in music the deep theology of the words. This is a hymn tune to become enthusiastic about and to encourage its use every Palm Sunday!

Another discovery was how a hymn may work best with a tune not printed above it. Hymn 387, "The Church of God a Kingdom is," has a decent enough tune, *St. Bavon*. But an English organist suggested, for Hymn 387, using the tune *Capel* (586), a 1906 arrangement by R. Vaughan Williams of a very old Sussex folk dance tune, which breathes new life into the magnificent text. This is a great hymn to use as an Offertory or during Communion on the Fourth Sunday in Lent, with the theme of the Church as our holy Mother, feeding us in the Eucharist, our participation in the glory of the new creation, the new Jerusalem.

Generally speaking, the opening hymn to a Liturgy, Morning Prayer, Evening Prayer or the Eucharist, should be a something that introduces us to our worship and gives praise to God. So we might begin on Trinity Sunday with the well known Hymn 266, "Holy, Holy, Holy!" A Sequence or Gradual hymn should, if possible, correspond to the theme of the Epistle or Gospel. On Trinity Sunday, Hymn 273, "Holy God, we praise thy Name," would work well. The Offertory Hymn should allow us to see that we are now returning creation to the Father, through the Son, in the Holy Spirit. Hymn 267 could be used. A Communion Hymn may often come from the section called "Holy Communion," hymns 189 to 213. Or a Communion Hymn could bring in the theme of our personal relationship with the Lord, such as 456, "My God, I love thee not because," or 471, "Rock of ages, cleft for me." The final hymn should send us on our way rejoicing, perhaps with something like 489, "Lord, dismiss us with thy blessing," or 287, "Give praise and glory unto God."

It can be creative to have some mix of various hymnodic cultures: patristic (#195 or 197), together with something evangelical, with the occasional German Lutheran chorale, such as # 3, or 332, and something English (#542 is both English and evangelical) and something Anglo-Catholic (599). The hymns cited here would not work in the same service, but are examples of hymnody from different historical periods and strands of churchmanship.

**Principles of Chanting** on p. 697 (small number at the bottom) is a section well-worth browsing through, if only to know that this section is here, for reference. The same is true for p. 698, **Directions for Anglican Chanting**, and p. 699, **Directions for Plainsong Chanting**. You will either need to know about these matters, or seek advice from those who do. When I had to learn how to sing the *Exsultet* on Easter Eve, a gifted organist-choirmaster showed me in a phrase a basic principle that opens up the whole *ouvre*. If one cannot gain basic mastery of something chanted, it is best to either delegate to a cantor, or say it, the principle being, "only do what you can do well." Simplicity is always a good default position.

**The Choral Service**, p. 699 The Ferial Preces (for Morning and Evening Prayer). This is the simple setting most often heard in our churches. On p. 701 are Suffrages after the Creed, again, for Morning and Evening Prayer.

**The Invitatory Antiphons**. p. 704, Hymns 603–606. At the bottom of the page it is noted that the chant for these antiphons should be the same as the Venite. The names associated with these are on the whole the composition of English cathedral choirmasters. *The 1940 Hymnal Companion*, begun by Canon Winfred Douglas, often has fascinating commentary on these and other texts.

**The Anglican chants for the Venite** in MP, p. 705, Hymns 607–610. For those who grew up in the Episcopal Church, some of these are quite familiar. Those who did not do so will come to love Anglican Chant, as what "sweetens the pie." Some Anglican chants composed in the 20th century ("the second renaissance in the English cathedral choir tradition") are world-class masterpieces. R. Vaughan Williams, Herbert Howells, Herbert Sumsion, Everett Titcombe, Edward Bairstow and Francis Jackson come to mind.

**Plainsong**, of course, being "music of the heart," is the enduring foundation of music in the Western Church, Anglican chant being an adaptation of it. We are blessed in our hymnal to have a rich array of Plainsong chant, much of it arranged by Canon Winfred Douglas, 1867-1943 (sometime Canon at St. Paul's Cathedral in Fond du Lac, Wisconsin) after he spent time in France with the Benedictine monks of Solesmes, studying the revival in Plainsong in the early 20th century. There is a portrait of Canon Douglas in the frontispiece of *The 1940 Hymnal Companion*. His enrichment of the music of the Episcopal Church is inestimable. For example, in 1933, "he published the *St. Dunstan Kyrial*, his compilation of 12 plainsong masses and other service music." (Dorothy Mills Parker, *The Living Church*) Usually, when we sing Hymn 563, "He who would valiant be," we use the tune *St. Dunstan's,* composed by Canon Douglas in 1917.

**The Plainsong Invitatory Antiphons and Venite for MP** are on pp. 706–707, Hymns 611–612.

**The Deum Laudamus**, both Anglican Chant and Plainsong settings, are on pp. 708–711, Hymns 613–622. It is sometimes claimed that St. Ambrose of Milan (340 -397 AD) wrote the Te Deum. The Gloria Patri is never added to the end, because the whole canticle is a doxology to the Trinity. The Te Deum should be used at MP only when there is a Gloria in excelsis in the Mass of the day. In other words, in Advent and Pre-Lent and Lent, excepting occasional feast days when the Gloria is used at Mass, the Te Deum would not be used. Use instead the Benedictus es, Domine, which comes next in the Hymnal.

**The Benedictus es, Domine**, with Anglican Chants only, is on p. 712, Hymns 623–626. This comes from the Apocrypha (Song of the Three Young Men, vss. 29-34). It is what Hananiah, Azariah and Mishael sang in the burning fiery furnace. and as noted above, it is used during penitential seasons when the Te Deum is omitted. When the Te Deum is omitted it is also possible to use the next canticle, the Benedicite, omnia opera Domine.

**The Benedicite, omnia opera Domine**, with Plainsong and Anglican Chants, is on pp. 713–715, Hymns 627–633. This Canticle comes right after the Benedictus es, Domine, from the Song of the Three Young Men, vss. 35–66, in the Apocrypha, "a series of exhortations for all creatures, animate and inanimate, to praise the Lord" (Oxford Commentary Bible, p. 209). I like to use this canticle at MP during Pre-Lent, starting on the Monday after Septuagesima Sunday. It is traditionally used at this time because in our hemisphere, creation is awakening, and the First Lesson at MP on this day is Gen. 1: 1-19. We begin reading Genesis on this morning, and this is not a coincidence. It was the old monastic tradition to read about creation at the onset of spring. Anglican teaching and hymnody is always very strong on creation. It is one of the excellent features of our 1943 Lectionary that it uses the themes of the times and seasons as the basis for the readings.

**The Benedictus** is on pp. 716–720, Hymns 634–641, with Anglican and Plainsong chants. The Benedictus is the climax of MP, and so should (nearly) always be favored. Use of the Gospel canticles from Luke (the Benedictus at MP, and the Magnificat and Nunc dimittis at EP) impress upon us the theme of every daily office: the Incarnation. The theme of every Sunday is the Resurrection. The theme of every other day is the Incarnation, a point further driven home by the use of the Angelus at 6 am, 12 noon and 6 pm.

**The Jubilate Deo**, on pp. 721–722, Hymns 642–646, can be used when MP needs to be shortened. It is also very suitable in the Eucharist, on Sundays or feast days (except in penitential seasons) as a psalm between the OT Lesson and Epistle, or as a sequence hymn between the Epistle and Gospel.

**The Magnificat**, on pp. 722–726, Hymns 647–658) is the Song of Mary, a "Gospel Canticle" from Luke. It is the climax of Evening Prayer, and therefore is the canticle that should normally be used after the First Lesson. Remember, the Daily Offices commemorate the Incarnation, and the Eucharist, the Paschal Mystery of Jesus' Death and Resurrection.

**The Cantate Domino** (Psalm 98), with Anglican Chant settings, is found on p. 727, Hymns 659–660. We sometimes use one of these settings for this psalm at Mass, after the OT Lesson (just before the Epistle).

**The Bonum est confiteri** (Psalm 92, vss. 1-4) is also useful at Mass, after the OT Lesson, just before the Epistle, and is on p. 728, Hymns 661–666.

Anglican Chant and Plainsong settings for **the Nunc dimittis** are pp. 729–730. This is the Song of Simeon, the Canticle that should normally be used after the Second Lesson at EP, since it is part of the Incarnation cycle.

**The Deus misereatur** (Psalm 67), on p. 731, Hymns 674–675, is useful after an OT Lesson at Mass (or for parishes that do not have an OT lesson at Mass, as a sequence hymn between the Epistle and Gospel), especially in Epiphanytide or Trinitytide.

Anglican Chants for **the Benedic, anima mea** (portions of Psalm 103). are, again, useful after the OT reading at Mass, or between the Epistle and Gospel, during seasons that use white or green. After using it for some weeks running, it becomes part of the parish repertoire. These chants are on p. 732, Hymns 676–679.

On p. 733 we find music for Occasional Canticles, Hymns 680–683, the Pascha nostrum (**Christ our Passover**). On Easter morning this replaces the Venite at MP, and may be used throughout the Octave in place of the Venite. We often use it after the OT Lesson at Mass. It is sometimes used at Mass after an opening hymn, in place of the Introit. At the Cathedral we plan to use 683 at Mass after the OT Lesson throughout Eastertide.

p. 735, Hymns 684–687 are intended for Thanksgiving Day, for a portion of **Psalm 147** to be used in place of the Venite at MP.

Here, on pp. 737–742, Hymns 688–700, are Anglican chants for the **psalms for the Burial of the Dead**. At our Sunday Masses this past Lent we used Hymn 697 (Psalm 130) after the OT Lesson.

**The First Communion Service**, John Merbecke's adaptation of Plainsong for the first PB of 1549, is on pp. 743–751, Hymns 701–707. This Mass setting is well known and used throughout the Anglican Communion. We use it during Pre-Lent, and for the first two-thirds of Trinitytide, along with a Plainsong Creed and Our Father.

**The Second Communion Service**, composed by Healey Willan in 1928, is on pp. 759–759, Hymns 708–713. This sturdy, modern setting caught on, and is well known and used in the U.S. and Canada. Willan was the organist at St. Mary Magdalene's in Toronto, so he named this Mass "Missa de Sancta Maria Magdalena." Note that this Mass includes (708) the people's responses in the Decalogue. We use this Mass in Christmastide and Epiphanytide, and in Eastertide, Ascensiontide, Whitsunday and Trinity Sunday, and at synods, with a Plainsong Creed and Our Father.

**The Third Communion Service** was composed by George Oldroyd in 1938, and is found on pp. 759–772, Hymns 714–718. This is a difficult Mass which requires a lot of practice and probably a choir, so one does not hear it very often. With a choir that can give leadership, or sing it without the congregation, it can be quite lovely.

**The Fourth Communion Service**, from ancient and medieval Plainsong, is on pp. 775–783, Hymns 719–724, and is known as the "Missa Marialis." We use this all through Advent and Lent. Plainsong, being "music of the heart," is easy to follow, and to sing, once heard a few times. There is something contagious about it. When we use other Mass settings, we always use the Plainsong Creed, # 720, and the Plainsong Our Father, # 722, both of which are very ancient. This setting is well known in Anglo-Catholic circles.

**The Responses to the Decalogue** are on pp. 783–784. We use the Decalogue at the Cathedral on the first Sunday of every month (transferring it to another Sunday, or omitting it, if there is a Litany in Procession, or a baptism or confirmation that day). We usually use the Hymns 701 or 708 as responses (Merbecke & Willan).

**Additional music,** on p. 784–794 give us Hymns 726–741: a Kyrie, the Gloria tibi, At the Presentation of the Alms and Oblations, the Sursum Corda, a Sanctus & Gloria in excelsis (including # 739, the very popular one that highlights the Celtic in us, *Old Scottish Chant*) and a sung Amen.

p. 795: Index of Service Music p. 796–798: Acknowledgments and Permissions p. 799: Subject Index of General Hymns p. 799–803: Topical Index p. 804–806: Liturgical Index, Hymns Suggested for the Services of the Church Year. This is very useful.

p. 807–810: Index of Authors, Translators, Sources p. 811–814: Index of Composers, Sources, Arrangers p. 815–818: Metrical Index. Every hymn tune has a meter. Take, for example, Hymn 387, "The Church of God a kingdom is, Where Christ in power doth reign…" The words are by Lionel B. C. L. Muirhead, written in 1899…a fabulous hymn for Lent IV, either at the Offertory, or during Communion…or a hymn for just about any Sunday or occasion. The tune, *St. Bavon*, is good enough, and has the meter printed at the top, in the middle: the letters "C.M." which stands for common meter. Any hymn that lists C.M. can be sung to any other hymn with common meter. As you can see from the Index, a lot of hymns have common meter. One of them is 586. A gifted English organist once pointed out how Hymn 387 is best sung with the tune 586, Capel, composed in 1906 by R. Vaughan Williams, inspired by a Sussex folk dance tune. Once you hear Hymn 387 sung to Tune 586, you will see that this is the perfect combination. The music lights up the text in a new way. The text, already theologically brilliant, is now even more joyful, radiant, confident, and even boisterous in the exuberance of God's love.

p. 819–821: Index of Tunes. If you look up the tune *Capel* here, you can see that it is 586.

p. 821: Hymns Suitable Also for Use as Anthems, anthems being what a choir or a schola could sing during an Offertory or Communion time.

p. 822–828: Index of First Lines. You may find yourself using this a lot.

**Supplement to the Hymnal 1940:** p. 829–857, Hymns 742–760: This is Supplement I, added in 1961, with a Liturgical Index on p. 830 that includes the new service music…some outstanding plainsong and new Anglican chants. Hymns 747–749 is the **5th Communion Service**, composed in 1957 by Leo Sowerby, then organist at the Cathedral of St. James in Chicago. The 5th Communion Service is easy for a congregation to learn. Since no Gloria in excelsis is provided for it, one may use the *Old Scottish Chant* or some other setting for the Gloria, or, use the Sowerby on Sundays when there is no Gloria.

**The 6th, 7th and 8th Communion Services** follow, along with a Martin Shaw Sanctus and Agnus Dei.

Then, Hymn 759 is a Nicene Creed, Mode V, often used in the summertime in parishes with a sung Liturgy. Hymn 720, the 9th century plainsong Creed, is quite solemn, and 759 is just a bit brighter.

**Supplement II**, inserted in 1976.

p. 859 is a list of alternate tunes for the hymns that are listed.

p. 860, Hymn 761, is an example of an alternate tune for the well-known hymn, "Rejoice, rejoice, believers!"

p. 861, Hymn 762A. The composer was Alastair Cassels-Brown, who haromonized this old Southern tune in 1974. Cassels-Brown was the Organist and Director of Music at the (then) Episcopal Theological School in Cambridge, Massachusetts. Who would guess that a composer at the world's most gnostic seminary would harmonize old Southern folk tunes? But he did, and God works this way, as we know, using the least likely people for work that needs to be done. We shall see, in the "Southern harmonies" which Cassels-Brown worked on, how Scotch-Irish and Appalachian tunes are…hauntingly beautiful. You can almost hear them being played on bag-pipes.

Hymn 767A. The tune "Holy Manna," another Southern harmony re-worked by Cassels-Brown in 1974. 767B has somewhat richer and fuller harmonics.

Hymn 770. the 1974 tune, *MacDougall*, for George Herbert's 1633 poem, "Let all the world in every corner sing…" My favorite musical rendition of this poem is by R. Vaughan Williams, who set Herbert's *Five Mystical Songs* to music. Vaughan William's "Let all the world" can be heard on You-tube.

Hymn 777A and 777B. Cassels-Brown's rendition of the Southern harmony *Charleston,* which we tried using some years ago as a Communion Hymn at a Synod Mass in Columbia. The "A" version is bare bones, little more than melody, and the "B" has richer, fuller harmonics. A magnificent tune for this great hymn.

Hymn 780. For years we have used this as a Processional at our Synod Masses. This is the great tune, always used in England, by Henry Purcell (1659-1695).

Hymn 782. *Amazing Grace,* America's quintessential hymn, makes it into our Hymnal.

Hymn 784 A & B, the Southern harmony, Landall, revisited by Cassels-Brown. I am not familiar with this, but want to hear it, and learn it.

Hymns 787–794. Modern Anglican chants, more material for a bucket list. The 20th century was outstanding for Anglican chant, and modern composers in the great cathedrals, but as the gnostic *Weltanschauung* settles in, the great lights are dimming and going out. Gnostics, ambivalent as they are about creation, and blocked as they are to the Holy Spirit, cannot produce great or even decent art in any form — music, art, sculpture, architecture, theater, literature or poetry. Everything is reduced to dissonance, shrieking, chaos, banality and mud.

Hymn 795. A great Plainsong *Te Deum*, easy for a congregation to learn.

Hymns 796–801. *Benedictus qui venit* for Communion Services 1–8. As you know, the *Blessed is he that cometh in the name of the Lord* was stripped from the Sanctus in 1552, to placate the Puritans. In our Liturgy it came back by way of the 1940 Hymnal, in this 1976 Supplement (and, a generation prior to that, in the Anglican and American Missals).

In conclusion, we are grateful to God for the 1940 Hymnal, widely recognized as one of the greatest ever produced, anywhere, in any age, because it is so robustly *catholic*. As the Supplements suggest, we need a new hymnal, to include magnificent modern compositions from the early 1980s such as the tune *Abbot's Leigh*, from the New English Hymnal (and other sources). The final hymn at our Cathedral's Synod Chrism Mass is usually the masterpiece, "Glorious things of thee are spoken," sung to the tune *Abbot's Leigh*. Another masterpiece of the 1980s is Herbert Howell's now famous tune, *Michael*, used for a variety of hymns.

# CANON LAW

For this section on Canon Law, we will be referencing Daniel B. Stevick's *Canon Law, a Handbook,* published by Seabury Press in 1965. If you can get this at a reasonable price on Amazon it is a worthy addition to your library.

Another worthwhile text is any version prior to 1967 of the *Constitution and Canons for the Government of the Protestant Episcopal Church in the United States of America.* It is not necessary to have this, but informative, since the Canons of the Diocese of the Holy Cross are rooted in these, as are the most of the canons of the jurisdictions of the Anglican Joint Synods and other continuing church bodies. It is possible to see that many of the same people, or communities of people, were part of the drafting of both the original Constitution and Canons of the Protestant Episcopal Church, and the Constitution of the United States of America.

The Canons of the Diocese of the Holy Cross are available on the website, www.dioceseoftheholycross.org.

**Aspects of Canon Law:** Canon Law is like an earthen vessel, containing the grace of God. St. Paul said in 2 Cor. 4: 7, "We have this treasure in earthen vessels." We may also think of canon law as a carton for eggs, shoes on one's feet, a channel for a river, a frame of reference, or a matrix, which holds us in place while God "performs the mercy."

The great Russian poet, Yevgeny Yevteshenko, who spent time in Stalin's gulags, said, "The purpose of politics is to protect love and motherhood." We could say the same of Canon Law. We want the flow of God's grace in the Church to be protected, channeled, enabled and made available.

In other words, we want to see the *perichoretic* relationship between Canon Law, Theology and Scripture. Psalm 119, the "Rosary of the Psalter" teaches us various aspects of what God's Law is, using the words law, statute, ordinance, precept, testimony, commandments, judgments, word and ways. Jesus fulfills this. He is the Law incarnate, the Word incarnate. He is grace-made-visible. Law and Grace, Law and Gospel, Geist und Amt (Spirit and Office, or, Charism and Structure), universal and local, are consubstantial and perichoretic.

St. Paul, in his epistles, usually begins with the **indicative** (the theological, the Gospel — what God has done in Christ). Then he goes on to the **imperative** (the moral, the ethical, the canonical — how we respond in the Spirit). We can see the dividing line in Romans at 12: 1; (in 1 and 2 Corinthians, the indicative and the imperative are intermingled); the dividing line in Galatians is 5: 1; in Ephesians it is 4: 1; in Philippians, 2. 12; in Colossians, 3; 1; In I Thessalonians the two are mixed; In 2 Thessalonians it is 3: 1; In the Pastoral Epistles, the two are mixed. Up to the dividing-line verse, most everything is indicative (the Gospel) and after the dividing line, everything is imperative (the moral, ethical and canonical)

There are two kinds of Canon Law in the Western Church:

(i) English Common Law, or case law, is based on cases as they arise. First live it, then put it on paper. If something is not expressly forbidden, it is permitted. In this system we can see the release of the human spirit and the release of charisms in the Body of Christ.

(ii) In French Code Law, there is an effort to anticipate all possible situations. Everything is put on paper first. In other words, we start with political process and, perhaps, bureaucratic wrangling. If something is not expressly permitted, it is forbidden. This system can be a dampener for creativity and innovation, and may help explain why the British, not the French, came out on top in North America in the 18th century.

We may now review four modes of governance in the Church (for which there can of course be overlaps):

(i) Magisterial (the Roman system, with its teaching magisterium centered in the Papacy)
(xi) Confessional (the system of the magisterial reformers, especially Luther and Calvin)
(xii) Congregational, with the local congregation deciding all matters of faith and practice
(xiii) Conciliar (the system of the undivided Church of the first millennium, and today, of all the Orthodox, and traditional, orthodox Anglicans. In Vatican II, Rome took some steps toward conciliarity, communion theology and *ressourcement,* a French word that means getting back to the sources — the consensus of the undivided Church)

**The Canons of the Diocese of the Holy Cross (DHC).** Here are some important features:

Canon 2.01 Synod consists of all bishops of the Diocese, all Presbyters and Deacons, and three Lay Delegates from each Parish. (others also attend: Anglican Church Women representatives, guests and observers).

Canon 2.04 in the absence of the Bishop, and if there is no Bishop Co-adjutor, the Standing Committee is the ecclesiastical authority of the Diocese. (A Co-adjutor Bishop has been elected by Synod with the right of succession, whereas a Suffragan Bishop is an assisting Bishop with no right of succession, unless he is elected as a Co-adjutor or as the Ordinary of the Diocese.

Canon 2.05 Normally, Synod deliberates and votes as one body. But there are occasions for "voting by orders," when Bishops, Clergy and Laity vote as separate houses, with a concurrent majority needed in each Order to decide a matter. Voting by Orders is done when electing bishops, amending or adding canons, or when requested by a Bishop, or 3 Clergy, or 3 Lay Delegates.

Canon 2.07 Voting by proxy is allowed at Synods, except in the election of a Bishop.

Canon 3.01 Synod is the legislative authority of the Diocese with respect to its temporalities. DHC parishes are assessed at 10% of their non-designated, non-capital income. Synod is entrusted with the responsibility of enacting, repealing or amending canons.

Canon 3.04 Upon recommendation of the Bishop and Standing Committee, Synod recognizes and seats new qualifying parishes as they join the Diocese.

Canon 5.01 The Standing Committee consists of the Bishop(s), and 4 Priests and 4 Lay Communicants of the Diocese.

Canon 5.02 The Standing Committee is the Bishop's council of advice. Between Synods, it exercises the powers of the Synod, except that it may not enact, repeal or amend Canons.

Canon 7 The Diocese is incorporated (in the State of South Carolina) and has a Board of Trustees who meet briefly at Synod.

Canon 8.01 This Marriage Declaration is to be signed by both parties

Canon 8.02 A Bishop or Priest may decline to solemnize any marriage.

Canon 8.03 Impediments and Consanguinity. It is good to know what some of these impediments are.

Canon 8.04 The prospective couple must be either bachelor or widower and maiden or widow.

Canon 8.05 Six months notice are needed for a wedding, and times of instruction.

Canon 8.06 There are to be at least two witnesses at a wedding and a proper record kept in the Parish Register.

Canon 9.01 A baccalaureate degree is required for ordination to the Priesthood and Episcopate.

Canon 9.03 One requirement for ordination is that neither the candidate nor his wife may be divorced and remarried, if the first spouse is still living.

Canon 10.05 Postulants write to the Bishop four times a year, during the Ember Seasons.

Canon 11 After Postulancy comes Candidacy, although in practice we blur the two and just have Postulancy. In the old days one became a Candidate half-way through Seminary, with a recommendation coming from the seminary faculty.

Canon 12 Examining Chaplains test for academic achievement, whereas the Standing Committee interviews for spiritual, moral and vocational aptitude.

Canon 13 the Diaconate–a man is a Deacon for one year before ordination to the Priesthood, although the Bishop can shorten that to six months for cause. A Deacon can be Minister in Charge of a Congregation, under the supervision of the Bishop or a neighboring Priest.

Canon 14.02 "No man shall be ordained to the Priesthood without a Title." Title here means a parish or mission in which to serve, or a post, as, say, a Chaplain or a Professor.

Canon 15 Of the Election of Bishops, for which voting at Synod is by Orders.

Canon 16 Of the Duties of Bishops. An Episcopal Visit to every Congregation is required at least once a year.

Canon 17.01 DHC parishes may each be members of Forward in Faith/North America.

Canon 17.02 Every Parish must have an Annual Parish Meeting, to approve financial statements from the previous year, to approve a budget for the coming year, to elect members to the Vestry in accordance with the Parish By-laws, to elect delegates to Diocesan Synod and to hear reports.

Canon 17.07 Parish affiliation with the Diocese of the Holy Cross is voluntary.

Canon 17.08 A Parish may be incorporated under the laws of the State in which it is located. The Rector is the President of the Corporation and Chairman of the Board of Directors (the Vestry).

Canon 18. Of Vestries. The Vestry is the governing Board of the Parish. The Rector is President of the Corporation, with the right to preside and vote at all meetings. the Senior Warden is the First Vice-President, the Junior Warden, the Second Vice-President. If the Rector resigns, retires or dies, the ecclesiastical authority of the Parish is the Bishop, who becomes the acting Rector. The Bishop can appoint a Minister-in-Charge (a priest, deacon or lay reader) to care for the parish until a new Rector is called.

The Vestry calls a Rector. The Rector then calls curates or assisting clergy, organists, youth leaders, secretaries, janitors, and anyone else who works in the Parish. He also dismisses them if need be. He may or may not consult with the Vestry on these matters; however, a good and effective Rector will always consult, and work hand-in-glove with his Vestry, and by every means possible, work as a team. One among several reasons for team work is that although the Rector calls, let us say, a Curate, the Vestry decides whether or not, or how much, to pay him. The same is true for organists, and others who work at the Church. The Vestry controls the purse strings, and so a thoroughly collaborative approach usually works best. That does not mean that a Rector should not provide leadership. It means the Rector will best lead in synch with the Vestry, with as much unanimous decision making as possible. And consensus can usually be built, if one brings people along with new initiatives with teaching and explaining and listening, and sometimes modifying, over time.

Canon 18.03. Every Parish has a set of By-laws. Simple, boiler-plate versions of parish By-laws are available at www.dioceseoftheholycross.org. There are certain common features in typical Anglican parish' By-laws, as minimum standards. Parishes can add to the minimum standards, or embellish them, as they find helpful.

Canon 18.05.b. The Rector appoints the Senior Warden. Other officers are elected by the Vestry. There is an old adage that the Senior Warden should be the Rector's best friend in the Parish. His role is to help represent the Rector to the Congregation. In some parish traditions, the Junior Warden, sometimes called the People's Warden, represents the Congregation to the Rector. He is often put in charge of buildings and grounds.

There is no canonical requirement about how long a Vestryman serves, or on what basis he might rotate. The Parish decides that in its By-laws.

Canon 19.01. To be a Rector, one must be canonically resident in the Diocese. Otherwise a serving priest would have the title Assisting Priest. A Curate must also be canonically resident in the Diocese. Rector and Curate are canonical titles. Whereas the Vestry has the charge of the temporalities of the Parish, the Rector has the charge of its spiritualities. He is to have access and control of all Parish buildings and property.

Canon 19.02. The Vestry calls a Rector (it does not hire one), in consultation with the Bishop, and with his approval.

Canon 19.03. A Rector has life-long tenure in the parish, and can only be removed for cause (again, pertaining to matters of orthodoxy and moral conduct) with the joint decision of Bishop and Vestry.

Canon 19.04. Two or more parishes may call the same Priest as their Rector.

Canon 19.05. The Bishop is the acting Rector of a Parish which is without one, and may place in charge a clergyman or Lay Reader. (Clergy from other jurisdictions who serve in our parishes are licensed by the Bishop, and can have the title of "Assisting Priest" or "Assisting Deacon." To be called as a Rector or Curate a clergyman must be canonically resident in the Diocese, so he would leave his former diocese, with a Letter Dimissory from his bishop, and join the new Diocese.).

Canon 20. Parishes are to tithe to the Diocese 10% of their non-capital, non-designated income. Parishes may petition the Bishop for relief. Payment on some basis is a condition of qualifying Lay Delegates to Synod.

Canon 21. Certain Parish Records and Reports are required: a Service Register book, Minutes of all Vestry and Parish Meetings, kept by the Clerk of the Vestry, and Financial records, kept by the Treasurer, which are to include Income and Expense Statements, Budget for the year, and Balance Sheet. Every year the Rector sends a Parochial Report to the Diocese, on a form provided by the Bishop.

Canon 22. Of Parish Property is one of our 1977 reforms. All parishes absolutely own their property in fee simple. The Diocese has no claims or interest in parish property, unless money is owed to the Diocese.

Canon 22.02. Parish churches are consecrated when they are debt free. Until then they are "Dedicated." Parishes must carry liability, casualty and comprehensive insurance on their properties. A number of our parishes, and the Diocese itself, use Church Mutual, a Lutheran company based in Murrell, Wisconsin.

Canon 23. Of Suspending Union with the Diocese. A Parish may be asked to leave, for cause, by consent of the Bishop and 2/3 of the Standing Committee, or 2/3 vote of Synod. This has never happened in the DHC, and it is exceedingly rare anywhere. A Parish may leave the Diocese by whatever procedure it sets up in its own By-laws. The only canonical requirement is that the Bishop be notified within 10 days of the decision.

Canon 24.01 and 24.01 Of Worship: the 1928 BCP is the standard, along with Missals and devotional manuals conforming to it. Our primary supplements are the *American Missal*, the *Anglican Missal*, the *Priest's Manual*, the *St. Augustine's Prayer Book*, the *Practice of Religion*, and we have also made use of a eucharistic lectionary supplement that came out in the early 60's, *Lesser Feasts and Fasts*, and Prayer Books prior to 1928, from anywhere in the Anglican Communion, especially the 1662 BCP of the Church of England.

Canon 24.03–the Eucharist is to be the principle service on Sunday morning if a priests is available.

Canon 24.04–the King James version of the Bible is what is to be used for all readings, except that, for the Psalter, we use the BCP version, translated in 1535 by Myles Coverdale, which is better for chanting.

Canon 24.05–the 1940 Hymnal is our standard, subject to modification by Diocesan Authority. We have parishes that supplement or even replace the *1940 Hymnal* with the *English Hymnal* and the *New English Hymnal*. Hymns are sometimes taken from the C of E's *Hymns Ancient and Modern*. The Rector of a parish is in charge of all music, and matters pertaining to music, even if he chooses to delegate this to a music director or organist.

Canon 25.01–Enactment, amendment and repeal of canons can only take place by a majority vote in each Order of the Diocesan Synod. This is an example of "voting by Orders." Written notice of the proposed change must be given at least two months prior to the Synod, and circulated no less than 1 month prior to the Synod.

As an appendix to our Canons there are forms for endorsement for those applying for postulancy for Holy Orders, a Promise and Oath of Conformity for ordinands, a Declaration of Intention for those preparing to marry. and a policy and procedures statement concerning sexual misconduct.

Note that our Canons do not have an Ecclesiastical Court or a procedure for indicting or trying clergy. It was thought to be unnecessary in 2004 when our Canons were written, because of our small size. Now that our G-4 jurisdictions are converging, (the other 3 of which have an Ecclesiastical Court) we will most likely be adopting or simply using their canons for a "Judiciary," when needed.

Our polity, as we inherited it from the Episcopal Church, "presents a `checks and balances´ aspect. Very few actions can be taken by any order in the Church without the consent of the others. The parish, diocese and the (archdiocese or province) are each centers of real power which must be held and exercised in awareness of the other two. In the colonial period, the parish replaced the diocese as the basic unit of the Church. Dioceses were, in effect, federations of parishes." (Stevick, *Canon Law)*

For further reading–Dr. Daniel Stevick, as noted, *Canon Law: a Handbook,* and also E. A. White & J. A. Dykman, *Annotated Constitution and Canons,* NY, Seabury, 1954

DHC Canons are based on those drafted by the late Canon Francis W. Read, for the Province of Christ the King. Canon Read was legal counsel for the American Church Union, and widely recognized as one of the foremost canonists of the Episcopal Church.

# BIBLIOGRAPHY

*American Missal, The* revised and expanded (Glendale, CO, Lancelot Andrewes Press, 2016). First Edition, 1931, by Morehouse Publishing Co.

*Anglican Breviary, The* (Mount Sinai, Long Island, NY, Frank Gavin Liturgical Foundation, Inc., 1955)

*Anglican Missal, The* in the American Version (Athens, GA, Anglican Parishes Association, first edition, 1947)

Benson, Richard Meux, *The War Songs of the Prince of Peace*, A Devotional Commentary on the Psalter (London, John Murray, 1901)

*Book of Common Prayer, The* 1928 Edition (New York, Church Pension Fund)

*Book of Common Prayer, The* 1662 Edition (Cambridge University Press, 2004, *amazon.com*)

*Constitution and Canons for the governance of the Protestant Episcopal Church in the United States of America,* Printed for the Convention, 1964

Davies, Robertson, *The Rebel Angels* (Toronto, Macmillan, 1981)

Dix, Dom Gregory, *The Shape of the Liturgy* (London, Dacre, 1945)

Lampburn, E. C. R., ed., *Ritual Notes,* 11th ed. (London, W. Knott & Sons Ltd., 1964)

Lozano, Neal, *Unbound* (Ada, MI, Chosen Books, 2010)

Loudovikos, Nikolaos, *The Church in the Making, An Apophatic Ecclesiology of Consubstantiality* (Yonkers, NY, St. Vladimir's Seminary Press, 2016)

*Manual for Priests, A,* 5th edition (Cambridge, MA, Society of St. John the Evangelist, 1970)

McCrum, Robert, Cran, William and MacNeill, Robert, *The Story of English,* (New York, Viking Penguin Inc., 1986)

Middleton, Arthur, *Restoring the Anglican Mind* (Leominister, Gracewing, 2008).

Newbolt, W. C. E., *The Church Catechism, The Christian's Manual,* in the *Oxford Library of Practical Theology,* ed. by W. C. E. Newbolt and the Darwell Stone (London, Longmans & Co., 1899)

Parker, Dorothy Mills, *The Living Church Oxford Commentary Bible* (Oxford University Press, 2004, amazon.com)

*St. Augustine's Prayer Book* (Athens, GA, Anglican Parishes Association. First edition, 1947)

Schmemann, Alexander, *The Eucharist, Sacrament of the Kingdom* (Crestwood, NY, St. Vladimir's Seminary Press, 1988)

Schmemann, Alexander, *For the Life of the World: Sacraments and Orthodoxy* (Crestwood, NY, St. Vladimir's Seminary Press, 1970)

Shepherd, Massey H., *The Oxford American Prayer Book Commentary* (New York, Oxford University Press, 1950)

Stevick, Daniel B., *Canon Law, A Handbook* (Greenwich, CT, Seabury Press, 1965)

White, E. A., & Dykman, J. A., *Annotated Constituion and Canons* (NY, Seabury, 1954)

Zizioulas, John D., *Being as Communion* (Crestwood, NY, St. Vladimir's Semimary Press, 1997)

www.ingramcontent.com/pod-product-compliance
Ingram Content Group UK Ltd.
Pitfield, Milton Keynes, MK11 3LW, UK
UKHW022215230426
12048UKWH00016BA/857